The Worlds between Two Rivers

The Worlds between Two Rivers

Perspectives on American Indians in Iowa *An Expanded Edition*

Edited by Gretchen M. Bataille, David Mayer Gradwohl, and Charles L. P. Silet

UNIVERSITY OF IOWA PRESS Ψ IOWA CITY

University of Iowa Press, Iowa City 52242

Copyright © 2000 by the University of Iowa Press

Printed in the United States of America

http://www.uiowa.edu/~uipress

The Worlds between Two Rivers was originally published by
Iowa State University Press in 1978.

The photographs in "The Red Earth People in 1905" first appeared in
the *Palimpsest* 55 (1974).

The publication of this book was generously supported by the
University of Iowa Foundation.

Printed on acid-free paper

Library of Congress Cataloging-in-Publication Data
The worlds between two rivers: perspectives on American Indians
in Iowa / edited by Gretchen M. Bataille, David Mayer Gradwohl,
and Charles L. P. Silet.— An expanded ed.
    p.   cm.
Includes bibliographical references and index.
Bibliography: p.
ISBN 0-87745-700-X (pbk.)
1. Indians of North America — Iowa.   I. Bataille, Gretchen M., 1944– .
II. Gradwohl, David M., 1934– .   III. Silet, Charles L. P.
E78.16 w67   2000
977.7'00497 — dc21   99-051647

00 01 02 03 04 P 5 4 3 2 1

Royalties from the sale of this book go to the Iowa State University
Achievement Fund for the Buffy Sainte-Marie Scholarship Fund for
American Indian Students.

This book is dedicated to the memory of
Richard Thompson

and to our children
Marc, Erin, Jane, Steven, Kathryn, Karin,
Scott, Kristin, Emily

and grandchildren
Justin, Austin, Alexandra, Kelsey, Hanna, Sara

with the hope that their generation will know
all of America's history

Contents

Preface to the Revised Edition

More than twenty years have passed since the original essays for this book were collected and published. Although some progress has been made toward achieving the goals of diversity and equity in higher education and the general social fabric in Iowa, many of the problems and misunderstandings that plagued American Indians in the past are still with us today. In the hope of further pursuing these goals and increasing an awareness of the on-going presence of American Indians into the twenty-first century, the University of Iowa Press invited the editors of *The Worlds between Two Rivers: Perspectives on American Indians in Iowa* to submit a revised edition of their book for publication. Beyond the originally-printed essays, some updated bibliographic information, and this preface, this expanded edition also includes two additional chapters. The first, by Maria Pearson of the Yankton Sioux tribe, discusses the issues surrounding the reburial of disinterred American Indian skeletal remains and the repatriation of these bones and cultural objects to the contemporary tribal people who carry on the heritage of their ancestors. The second new contribution, by Lance Foster of the Ioway tribe, deals with the native people from whom the State of Iowa took its name. These two essays not only express the continuing American Indian presence in Iowa but also help non-Indian people to better understand those Iowans who represent the state's first nations.

As one might expect, there have been both continuities and changes since the first edition of this book was published. The American Indian Symposium held at Iowa State University, for which many of the original essays were prepared, began in 1971 and has continued throughout the ensuing years, making it the oldest ongoing event focused on cultural diversity and minority concerns on that campus. In the year 2000, the American Indian Symposium will sponsor the twenty-seventh annual Richard Thompson Memorial Lecture, named after the selfless individual who met a senseless death in Vietnam while serving as a non-combatant civilian medical worker. Rick's spirit is still a guiding light to those who work for the attainment of equality and dignity for all human beings.

During the 1970s, the American Indian Symposium spawned the United Native American Student Association (UNASA), which still functions at ISU along with the more recently established American Indian Rights Organization (AIRO) and the American Indian Science and Engineering Society (AISES). The American Indian Studies Program at ISU, another outgrowth of the annual symposium, still offers an interdepartmental undergraduate minor through the College of Liberal Arts and Sciences (formerly the College of Sciences and Humanities). Limited resources and staffing for American Indian Studies, however, have not allowed the program to reach its full potential in furthering ISU's stated goal of greater diversity on campus, so some of the challenges and problems articulated in the 1971 American Indian Symposium are still forces to be contended with today at ISU and, to be sure, throughout the larger American society.

American Indians living in Iowa today still grapple with many of the issues addressed in the original essays. Among these concerns are relevant education for their youth, retention of their children in schools, general health care and assistance for their elderly, representation of their political views on the state and federal levels, tribal factionalism at the local level, freedom to engage in traditional religious practices, access to jobs in or near their communities, and equitable treatment within the various legal systems to which they are accountable. As more and more elders pass away, some American Indians worry about losing their linguistic, social, and cultural heritage. They endeavor to preserve this heritage not only through traditional means, such as storytelling, song, and dance, but also with tape recorders, camcorders, and computers.

Perhaps the most far-reaching and complicated changes for American Indians in this region during the past twenty years have been connected to the establishment of gambling casinos by the Omaha, Winnebago, and Meskwaki (today's preferred spelling of the tribal name). The Meskwaki Casino complex just off Highway 30 near Tama and Toledo, for example, presently includes not only extensive gambling halls, but also a gas station, a hotel, and a huge theater area that attracts nationally-known musicians and entertainers. A large number of Meskwaki people have returned to the settlement to find employment at the casino complex and to avail themselves of new housing and medical facilities. Others enjoy the convenience of gambling activities that far exceed the traditional games like lacrosse or plum-pit dice tossed around in a basket. Not surprisingly, given the information on tribal factionalism included in several of this book's original essays, there is a lack of consensus on whether the casinos are a positive or negative factor in American Indian communities. While some Native Americans see the casinos as sources of tremendous economic opportunity, assistance to community housing, health, and educational programs, and access to the idealized "great American dream," others see them as further intrusions of foreign elements into their communities and perhaps the final threat to their linguistic, historical and cultural heritage. Tim Giago, publisher of the *Lakota Times*, recently remarked: "Whether Indian gambling turns out to be the new buffalo or the road to termination for the long-suffering Indian people depends on how they create and accept the new standards expected of them by the Indian nations who have turned their backs on gaming. The lessons to be learned from the traditional and spiritual leaders must be observed and adhered to or assimilation and acculturation will happen to the Indian people from within." This prediction is certainly one that must be pondered carefully as Indian communities, increasingly asserting their legal sovereignty, determine their own destinies. As Giago emphasized: "For one of the first times since 1492, the fate of the Indian people is on their own hands."

Community-based schools are one institution which may allow American Indians to offset the adverse impacts of casinos upon their native traditions. American Indian communities are much more in charge of their schools than they were thirty years ago. After long legal battles in court, for example, the Meskwaki were finally successful in wresting control of their settlement school from the Bureau of Indian Affairs. Now run by an Indian-controlled school board, the school has the option of integrating Meskwaki history, culture, and language into the overall curriculum. Plans are in place to begin construction on a new school building to house classes from kindergarten through the eighth grade; tribal members hope to eventually extend the program through the twelfth grade. Some Meskwaki also envision the construction of a cultural heritage center that would exhibit not only historic artifacts but also works by contemporary tribal artists. A museum shop at this proposed center would be the logical distribution point for sketches, prints, watercolor and oil paintings, beadwork, finger weaving, wood carvings, musical tapes and compact disk recordings, and literary works being produced by native artists, musicians, and writers. Taking a cue from American Indian community heritage centers elsewhere around the United States, tribal museums in Iowa could also sponsor storytelling events, language classes, and other programs to help perpetuate their cultural traditions into the twenty-first century and beyond.

New initiatives for preserving and assuming management of American Indian culture history have also arisen since the passage of the federal Native American Grave Protection and Repatriation Act (NAGPRA) in 1990. With the return of many artifacts from museums and other institutions across the country, American Indians are in a better position to control the interpretation of their particular histories and to plan relevant museums or cultural centers on their own terms. While NAGPRA unquestionably shook up the professional communities of historians, museum directors, anthropologists, and archaeologists in terms of the "ownership" and "patrimony" of cultural items, it can be argued that this legislation also opened up many positive opportunities for tribal research, the training and participation of American Indians in the venture of historical scholarship, the sensitizing of non-Indian professionals to Native American knowledge systems, and — most importantly — the cooperation of professional scholars and lay people in the tasks of cultural and historical preservation and interpretation. The work of Lance Foster and Maria Pearson, and their essays here, exemplify these matters.

Of the original contributors to this book, four are deceased: Gary Koerselman, Reuben Snake, Adeline Wanatee, and Bertha Waseskuk. Shortly before he died, Reuben Snake told his life's story to Jay C. Fikes and it was posthumously published under the title *Reuben Snake, Your Humble Serpent: Indian Visionary and Activist* (Santa Fe, New Mexico: Clear Light Publishers, 1996). Adeline Wanatee stepped over to the other side in 1996; three years earlier she was honored by becoming the first Native American to be inducted into the Iowa Women's Hall of Fame. The passing of Bertha Waseskuk was a great loss to the tribe; her essay in the first edition of this book has been acknowledged as a valuable expression of Meskwaki historical knowledge that has been handed down through the generations by word of mouth.

Other essayists have continued their professional careers and concerns with diversity issues. Joseph Hraba remains a Professor of Sociology at Iowa State University, teaches classes on ethnicity in the United States, and conducts research on ethnicity, economic, and health issues not only here but in Europe and Asia. Owana McLester-

Greenfield teaches literature at Simpson College, in Indianola, Iowa, and is the owner of the Mastery Co. which specializes in communications training; in 1993 she received the Outstanding Adult Educator of Iowa award. Donald Wanatee still resides at the Meskwaki Settlement with his wife and some of his children and grandchildren. He completed his Masters of Social Work degree at the University of Iowa and subsequently served the Meskwaki as a professional social worker and as the tribe's executive director.

Four of the original essayists have left Iowa for positions elsewhere. Donald Graham lives in Aberdeen, South Dakota, where he is employed by the Indian Health Service. Michael Husband left Morningside College in Sioux City to work in historical museums both in Arizona and Colorado. After leaving Iowa, Fred McTaggart taught at Western Michigan University in Kalamazoo. He operates a business there writing health-care-related articles for hospitals. In 1993 he wrote a review of Ray Young Bear's *Black Eagle Child* for the *Annals of Iowa*. L. Edward Purcell lives in Lexington, Kentucky, where he is a free-lance writer of educational references; he is the author or co-author of sixteen books on historical topics.

The lives of the three editors, who likewise contributed essays to the book, also reflect continuity and change. Since the first edition of this book was published, Gretchen Bataille has had administrative positions at Arizona State University in Tempe, the University of California at Santa Barbara, and Washington State University in Pullman. She presently lives in Chapel Hill, where she is senior vice president of Academic Affairs for the University of North Carolina system. She continues to teach courses on American Indian literature and oral traditions, and has two grandsons to listen to her own stories linking the past to the present. After thirty-two years at ISU, David Gradwohl took an early retirement, is now a professor emeritus, still teaches a course on American Indian ethnology, pursues research on the relationship of material culture and ethnicity, and finds time to enjoy and help enculturate his four granddaughters. Charles L. P. Silet continues teaching, research, and writing as a professor of English at ISU; he has published widely on the subjects of contemporary fiction, culture, and film.

As we enter the new millennium, we are confident that further progress will be made toward achieving the goals of diversity and equity in Iowa and in American society in general. As the children and grandchildren of our generation face these issues, we are hopeful that they will do so with an inclusive knowledge of various cultural traditions in America in addition to a commitment to strive with others in building a shared future that nurtures mutual human understanding.

David Mayer Gradwohl
Ames, Iowa 1999

Introduction

In 1971 the Iowa State University Institute on National Affairs was devoted to the topic "Indians: First Americans Last." That institute brought into focus various campus and statewide interests and concerns that had been building up during the turbulent sixties. An immediate outgrowth of the 1971 symposium was the formation of a campus group called the United Native American Student Association (UNASA). Subsequently a Committee on American Indian Studies was appointed by the Office of the Vice President for Academic Affairs. Since then, UNASA and the Committee on American Indian Studies have sponsored five spring symposia on campus: "Symposium on the American Indian in the University" (1973), "Indian Perspectives on Iowa: Education, Spiritual Freedom, and Social Responsibility" (1974), "Iowa's Heritage: The Indian Citizen's Perspective on the Land, the People, and the Law" (1975), "American Indian Perspectives on the Bicentennial" (1976), and "Voices and Images: Understanding through American Indian Arts" (1977). These programs have been supported by funds from the University Committee on Lectures, the Government of the Student Body, the Iowa Board for Public Programs in the Humanities, the Iowa American Revolution Bicentennial Commission, Care and Share in Cedar Rapids, and the Barnes Publishing Company.

In this book we have attempted to bring together the important issues raised in the five symposia held on the ISU campus. This volume is focused on American Indians (or Native Americans as many prefer to be designated) in Iowa and will, it is hoped, provide some insights into an area where current and accurate materials are generally lacking. Some of the chapters presented here were taken from papers and lectures delivered at the 1974 symposium. Others were written specifically for this volume and one was formerly in *The Indian Historian*. The chapters selected intentionally reflect the widest spectrum of views: those of Native Americans and those of Euro-Americans, those of lay people and those of professional educators, social scientists, and humanists. Readers of this volume will note that the definition of issues as well as the perception of "facts" will differ somewhat in the writings of the various authors. That is to be expected. Citizens of Iowa come from different ethnic and historic backgrounds and they, to some degree, continue to live in different worlds.

"Solutions" to contemporary "problems" cannot arise out of the homogenization of people's differing perceptions of themselves as individuals or as members of various groups. These "solutions" are neither quick nor easy. Unfortunately they cannot, in our opinion, be found in this or any other single volume. On the other hand, potential solutions can evolve from a basis of mutual understanding and a willingness to tolerate diversity. It is toward that objective that this volume is aimed.

It is our hope that readers of this book will join us in the circular path, attempting to gain needed insights into Iowa, bounded by the Mississippi and Missouri, and its people who live in the "worlds between two rivers."

It is impossible to thank individually all the students and colleagues who have worked on the spring symposia and the many Native Americans who have participated so generously in helping to develop our campus programs. In addition to the organizations mentioned above, however, we wish to thank the following for their assistance and encouragement in preparing this book: Dr. Daniel J. Zaffarano (Dean of the Graduate College and Vice-President for Research), Dr. Wallace A. Russell (Dean of the College of Sciences and Humanities), the Sciences and Humanities Research Institute, Dr. Donald R. Benson (Chairman of the Department of English), and Dr. George M. Beal (former Chairman of the Department of Sociology and Anthropology). We are especially grateful for the assistance and patience of Gertrude Burrell of the Iowa State University Press during the preparation of the final manuscript.

The sources for the quotations appearing before each chapter are: Grant MacEwan, *Tatanga Mani, Walking Buffalo of the Stonies*, Edmonton, Alberta: M. J. Hurtig, Ltd., 1969; *Chicago Sun Times*, 17 Nov. 1968; Joseph K. Howard, *Strange Empire*, New York: Morrow and Co., 1952, p. 8; Francis La Flesche, *The Middle Five*, Madison: University of Wisconsin Press, 1963, p. xx; *Autobiography of Black Hawk as Dictated by Himself for Antoine LeClair*, edited by J. B. Patterson, Iowa City: Historical Society of Iowa, 1933; *South Dakota Review*, Summer 1971, John Milton (ed.), "Coming Back Home"; Chief Luther Standing Bear, *Land of the Spotted Eagle*, Boston: Houghton-Mifflin, 1933, p. xix; Nancy Lurie, *Mountain Wolf Woman*, Ann Arbor: University of Michigan Press,

1966, p. 87; Chief Luther Standing Bear, *Land of the Spotted Eagle*, Boston: Houghton-Mifflin, 1933, p. 248; Virginia Irving Armstrong, *I Have Spoken*, Chicago: Sage Books, 1971, p. 183; John Neihardt, *Black Elk Speaks*, Lincoln: University of Nebraska Press, 1961, pp. 279–80; Vine Deloria, Jr., *God Is Red*, New York: Grosset & Dunlap, 1973, p. 301; Virginia Irving Armstrong, *I Have Spoken*, New York: Pocket Books, 1972, p. 130. Benjamin K. Rhodd, in Brian O.K. Reeves and Margaret A. Kennedy, eds., *Kunaitupi, Coming Together on Native Sacred Sites, Their Sacredness, Conservation, and Interpretation*, Calgary: Archaeological Society of Alberta, 1993, p. 57; and Watchemonne ("the Orator"), in Martha Royce Blaine, *The Ioway Indians*, Norman: University of Oklahoma Press, 1995, pp. 154–65.

Finally we wish to dedicate this book to the memory of Richard Thompson, a former student at Iowa State University, a moving force in the 1971 symposium, and a cofounder of the United Native American Student Association.

Gretchen M. Bataille
David Mayer Gradwohl
Charles L. P. Silet

The Worlds between Two Rivers

1 American Indian Literature
Contexts for Understanding

FRED MCTAGGART

In this chapter and in his book *Wolf That I Am*, Fred McTaggart acknowledges that Indian literature is one way of knowing the culture, but he explains the inherent difficulties of non-Indians studying the literature of Native Americans. Because of the stereotypes encouraged by much American literature, as well as the inability of non-Indians to recognize the teaching functions and sacredness of most American Indian literature, it is necessary to approach the teaching of such literature with an openness to new techniques and a sensitivity to the cultures from which the literature comes. The study of American Indian literature provides an alternative perspective to the images of the Native American fostered by the White culture. In Chapter 2, Charles L. P. Silet discusses the image projected by the motion picture industry and in Chapter 3, L. Edward Purcell deals with the biased picture appearing in textbooks. Both offer a sharp contrast to the images that appear in Indian literature.

Oh, yes, I went to the white man's schools, I learned to read from school books, newspapers, and the Bible. But in time I found that these were not enough. Civilized people depend too much on man-made printed pages. I turn to the Great Spirit's book which is the whole of his creation. You can read a big part of that book if you study nature. You know, if you take all your books, lay them out under the sun, and let the snow and rain and insects work on them for a while, there will be nothing left. But the Great Spirit has provided you and me with an opportunity for study in nature's university, the forests, the rivers, the mountains, and the animals which include us.
— Tatanga Mani, Stoney

From Cooper to Barth, the American Indian plays an important role in American literature. From our literary anthologies, we can construct a detailed, albeit distorted, portrait of the Euro-American's mythical Indian — stoic and feathered.[1] Our literary Indian has keen ears to hear the breaking of twigs in the forest, but he has no voice, singing no songs and telling no stories.

Those people who have had contact with American Indians know better. The Indian does perhaps have keen ears and is often silent; on certain occasions he might wear feathers. But he has a voice that can be clearly heard at powwows, ranging up and down the scale. These chants are meaningless only to those who have no ears to hear. To the traditional native American, the voice plays a very special role. When Black Elk "sends a voice," it is not a literary game but an attempt to communicate in the deepest sense with the powers of the universe. N. Scott Momaday says, "It seems to me that in a certain sense we are all made of words; that our most essential being consists in language."[2] The telling of stories and the singing of songs is central to traditional Native American culture. Each tribe has a literature that goes back to the very beginning and expresses the essence of what it means to be a member of that tribe and a human being. Among many peoples, these old stories and songs are still viable parts of a living culture. They are rich in implication and have the power to recreate an ancient and a not-so-ancient past when man lived in harmony with all the creatures of the universe. When fully understood, these stories and songs have the grace, beauty, eloquence, and universality that is expected of all great literature.

Yet, in our literary anthologies, the American Indian remains silent. Literary scholars who will argue that any "truly educated" person should be familiar with *Gilgamesh, Beowulf,* or the *Iliad* will readily admit their own ignorance of the classics of the North American continent — the Walum Olum of the Delawares, the Dekanawida of the Iroquois, the Night Chant of the Navajo. In recent years, Momaday, a Kiowa, and James Welch, a Blackfoot, have gained recognition as contemporary writers. Yet too often their novels and poems are read as social commentary rather than as literature. In Momaday's *House Made of Dawn* and Welch's *Winter in the Blood,* critics reconfirm their mythical image of the alienated Indian — destitute, abused, and on the verge of suicide and cultural extinction. Yet they seem unwilling or unable to look for the literary qualities that they expect in other imaginative works. Momaday's *The Way to Rainy Mountain,* which is closer to the Native American tradition in style and spirit, is seldom recognized as a major work.[3]

Such ignorance of Native American literature is unfortunate but understandable. The Euro-American stereotypes have kept us from a true knowledge of Native Americans and their culture. The insights of anthropologists and historians, when accurate, are hidden away in scholarly volumes. The many volumes of story and song texts, collected in the early part of this century, are presented as anthropological and linguistic data. Even though Franz Boas, Paul Radin, and Alfred Kroeber were sensitive to literary qualities, their work is primarily oriented toward anthropological concerns and is not well known by literary scholars. As they pointed out, American Indian literature has unique qualities and is not easily understood by those of an alien culture.

The most important problem is that the traditional stories are in native languages known to only a handful of White Americans. Even Boas and Radin realized their inadequacy as translators. And American Indians are reluctant and often unable to translate stories that they insist cannot be separated from the language in which they were given by the Creator. Translating the story changes it and robs it of much of its mystery and power to recall the ancient past, which exists in language as well as in memory. Only the original words, used as they have been used for centuries, can recreate past experiences that are powerful and sacred.

Ordinarily only the stories that are the least powerful and meaningful are passed along to translators. Hence, our collections of Native American literature generally consist of the worst and not the best examples of stories and songs. And even these examples are often incomplete. Many American Indians are reluctant to pass along references to bodily functions or supernatural powers that a White audience is likely to consider objectionable or unchristian. They understandably do not want to foster even more misunderstanding and stereotyping. And, of course, there are many words and actions that simply cannot be translated adequately into English. I was told that in a Mesquakie story about a Wolf and a Raccoon, there is one word that describes the act of the Raccoon in pushing bark off a tree to the Wolf waiting below. It is a word with many beautiful meanings, none of which can be understood even vaguely in English.

Any literature is difficult to translate; a person must be inside a culture to understand all the nuances and an American is handicapped even when reading the English of Yeats or Joyce. Indian languages are particularly difficult, partially because nearly all functions of the language have literary qualities, implying subtle, complex relationships.

In addition to the difficulty in translating stories from one language to another, there is the problem of translating them from an oral to a written medium. Although some texts, such as the Walum Olum, were recorded in some way through writing or pictographs, most of the stories are oral. They are to be told in a dramatic context that is nearly always destroyed by the presence of the alien collector. Early collectors laboriously copied the texts in a phonetic syllabary, a process that slowed the narration and robbed it of its dramatic elements. In the age of the tape recorder, many Native Americans are reluctant to record stories, feeling rightly that the tape can capture only the dead aspects of the story and the language. Few collectors are ever able to witness a story in its native context; many are uninterested or unwilling to recognize that this oral context is important. And even when the collector shares the dramatic experience, there is the extremely difficult problem of translating this oral experience to the printed page. Obviously a great deal more than a literal transcription is necessary to provide an adequate translation for a public that is generally ignorant of the ways of oral cultures.

The third problem is that these Native American stories are based on a concept of literature that is foreign to most White literary scholars. When I went to Tama, Iowa, to talk to people about Mesquakie literature, I went with preconceptions about the beauty of literature. And I was instantly rebuked: "There are many things about White culture we find beautiful too, but our stories have a purpose — a very definite purpose — and that purpose is to teach." All are teaching stories, even those that make us laugh about bodily functions; but they are not didactic in the manner of Pope or Dryden. The stories are complex cultural truths. What they teach cannot be summed up in a word or a sentence but must be experienced again and again as a story. They are important to Mesquakies as a way of holding together a powerful culture. They teach one what it means to be a Mesquakie and how one is to relate to ancestors and relatives. This teaching is for children and it is also for adults. A story is a piece of universal truth and a person might well measure his age and wisdom by the number of stories he knows.

Mesquakies told me that they could not tell me some stories because they were sacred, and I did not understand. The religion that I learned seeks converts. My sacred stories are in the Bible for anyone to see for any reason. But I could not understand the Mesquakie definition of "religion" and "sacred." I went to church one day a week; the rest of the week I lived. As a Mesquakie man told me, "We exercise our religion every day in everything that we do." The Mesquakie sacred stories are *functional* to their culture and hence are not intended for those who do not understand that culture. They provide religious truths that are to be used in everyday life, and they are told in a context. In a very poor early morning TV movie, an American Indian was invited to a cocktail party in a city and asked by the White guests to "do a rain dance; do a war dance." And he said, "I didn't know you wanted it to rain; I didn't know you wanted me to be angry. I am not an entertainer; I take these things seriously, and if I am going to do a rain dance, it's because I want it to rain; and if I do a war dance, it's because I am angry." It was a poor movie but a good insight: the stories are sacred because they have a function. This function is essential and as sacred as food. The stories are medicine. You go to a story when you need the story and when you are ready to learn from it. The story can make you whole.

A Navajo woman told me that she went to her grandfather to get some stories she has since published in a collection. He knew what she wanted them for, but he was very reluctant to agree to it. Finally, after two years, he was convinced that she wanted the stories for herself and that she had a need for them. Only then was he willing to give them to her and let her publish them in a book.

Stories concern events that have happened to a people in the past of waking life and in dreams and visions. These things are an important part of history and they are true and real. When a raccoon and a wolf meet in the woods, it is not merely to entertain us, but to teach us about the past and about our lives today. The animals were here many years before we were and they have something to teach. We need to know these animals, their stories, and the promises made among plants and animals and human beings and our creators as to the harmony and balance set up when our universe was created.

Stories are to be told on certain occasions, usually in winter. We have the romanticized notion of people sitting around campfires telling stories, and the notion is probably valid but not for the reasons we think. The fire on a winter evening has certain implications and certain powers that make it appropriate for telling stories. It is the time and place for reflections.

The final problem is that the stories are communal creations. They were not written by an individual author showing off his sense of aesthetics. The stories have been created by generations of people who have told stories because they know the teachings that are involved and because they want to share them. There are many different approaches to storytelling. Some tribes, such as the Mesquakie, tell stories in a very condensed form; stories get shorter as details are dropped over the years. Other tribes, such as the Ojibwas, elaborate at length and fill in many details. But there is little real difference. When stories are condensed, it is because a great deal is supposed to take place in the mind — images, ideas, and actions that the teller takes for granted his audience will know. The text on the page cannot catch all those nuances. What is not said is sometimes more important than what is said, and, of course, that is true of all great literature. Because most of us are not familiar with these cultural allusions, there are things we miss. Many Native Americans probably feel non-Indians have no right knowing some of these things, that they are a private part of the culture that is not to be shared. But I think there are universal truths that can and should be shared to a certain degree, as dances are shared at the powwow. In a secular version that does not desecrate the sacred functions, the traditional story can share teachings with people of all cultures.

I think it is obvious that Native American literature cannot be studied in a vacuum. If you are not a member of an Indian culture, you have to bring with you a great deal of knowledge about that culture. That is very difficult. If the Native American literature is on the printed page, that means commentary and sometimes footnotes that are cumbersome and hard to follow. And they get in the way of the literature. We have the same problem in studying early European literature. Readers need to know certain things about the culture to understand the literature, but it is difficult to bring these things in without interfering with the beauty and the function of literature.

So the problem is trying to find a context in which Native American literature can be presented. Dennis Tedlock in his book *Finding the Center* tries to catch the *performance* of Zuni narratives and the oral qualities by translating them as poetry. Through the printed line and typographical devices, he tries to show pauses, inflections, pace, and tone. To a large extent the book is successful. Chuck Storm, a Northern Cheyenne who taught two semesters at the University of Iowa, has attempted to provide in *Seven Arrows* interpretations of stories that can be understood by a non-Indian audience. To an extent his work is successful, although some Cheyenne are unhappy with the illustrations and feel that he told too much about their sacred traditions.[4]

An attempt to use modern media to provide a context for oral literature resulted in the animated film *Falling Star* by Sue Morton and Kay Miles, who felt that film was the best method to capture the oral quality of the literature and to avoid the problems of translation. In film there is a visual language with which we are all familiar. There are certain images — universal images — that people can identify with that go beyond language. The film is narrated, but there was a feeling when it was being made that perhaps narration was not needed, that the story should be carried by its images alone. Film, especially animated film, has a close connection with our fantasy life, with our dreams and visions. It is, perhaps, a contemporary version of an oral storytelling situation. At least that is what the filmmakers intended — to find a medium that could present a sacred story in a context in which it could be appreciated by any kind of audience, but especially by non-Indians. The story *Falling Star* is a simple one that is found in many collections of Native American stories. This particular version is taken from George Bird Grinnell's book *By Cheyenne Campfires.*[5] These stories were translated into English, so a great deal was lost, and the film directors recognized this. They did not take the story directly. They thought about it. They talked to people about it. They studied American Indian culture and art to try to find their own version.

This example presents an interesting challenge for using film, not in an ethnographic way, but creatively, attempting to transmit the sense, the spirit of one culture to another, moving the oral tradition right onto film. Film is a medium that can solve some of the problems we have had in the past. But one of the major problems in film is the concept of art and literature. It is based on the written word that one person read and interpreted; it is not based on a long oral tradition of wise teachers. It is not at all communal in that respect. Film is communal in terms of an audience, but Indian stories are not necessarily told to a big audience. Sometimes the stories are told to the members of one family at one time or maybe just to one child at one time. But the stories are communal in that they are created anonymously and owned by the people.

The film also raises the problem of symbolism. The images in the film are meant as natural symbols, but in the original Cheyenne story I doubt that they would be considered symbols — at least in the same way. As a Cherokee man in Chicago said, "People say the Earth is a Mother symbol. It's not a symbol; it *is* our Mother." The relationship between people and animals is set up in stories and in history. But the only way non-Indians have of understanding these relationships is by calling them symbols and saying that they represent something. Our view of the universe is egocentric — one person sees all these things and everything represents one state of mind. I think the consciousness represented in the original stories is broader and more abstract.

Film cannot totally bridge the gap between cultures, but it does offer a more viable way of attempting to move from one culture to another than the written word does. Editing Native American oral material for consumption by non-Indians is two steps removed from its source, first by the process of writing down the oral literature and second by translating the transcription into another language. By and large the nuances of language do not translate well. Perhaps by using images, by using film, some of the problems can be minimized, if not eliminated. The motion picture is a more fluid medium, which allows for an easier transformation.

There is a literalness to film that can also help to minimize the problems inherent in literary symbolism. That is, take a scene in which someone in a folktale takes on properties of an animal, one that is merely symbolic in literary terms. In the oral story that transformation is meant to be literal and on film that transformation can be made literal. You can turn something into something else. Perhaps that is a way of using film to fulfill the function of the oral story. The potential still exists for creating imagery that is universal, and the possibility of films doing that is extremely exciting. There are obviously still some enormous problems. Do you include narration? Does the narration provide an added dimension in any way? Does the narration, which after all is nothing but a bit of writing being read, move the story ahead?

One of the specific problems present in Native American tales involves the notion of living with animals. It is not something that comes very easily to many people anymore. The vast majority of people living in the United States see animals in cages or on television, but seldom in real life. Even the notion of living with nature is foreign. We air-condition our buildings, we heat our buildings, we hermetically seal ourselves off from the elements. I think it now requires an intellectual effort to imagine another kind of life. We must think about it instead of instinctively realizing, for example, that the porcupine has sharp quills and that it would be difficult to pick one up or kill it with our bare hands. And in the process of intellectualizing, we distance ourselves from a direct emotional involvement. When you begin to think like this, it is possible to see just how far apart the two cultures are. We are talking about an entirely different view of the world.

When we watch the sacred dances, we must see something not just beautiful or entertaining, although the dances are unquestionably both, but we must see the spiritual significance of the ritual, and we must then move beyond merely being a spectator and become identified with the experience. The very nature of such a process suggests the distance we still have to go to understand the stories and wisdom of the Native American.

NOTES

1. For a full discussion of images of the American Indian in American literature, see Richard Slotkin, *Regeneration through Violence* (Middletown, Conn.: Wesleyan University Press, 1973).

2. N. Scott Momaday, "Man Made of Words," *Indian Voices* (San Francisco: Indian Historian Press, 1970).

3. N. Scott Momaday, *The Way to Rainy Mountain* (Albuquerque: University of New Mexico Press, 1969); N. Scott Momaday, *House Made of Dawn* (New York: Harper & Row, 1968); James Welch, *Winter in the Blood* (New York: Harper & Row, 1974).

4. Dennis Tedlock, *Finding the Center* (New York: The Dial Press, 1972); Hyemeyohsts Storm, *Seven Arrows* (New York: Harper & Row, 1972).

5. George Bird Grinnell, *By Cheyenne Campfires* (New Haven, Conn.: Yale University Press, 1926).

2 The Image of the American Indian in Film

CHARLES L. P. SILET

In this chapter, Charles Silet examines the origins of some of the film images of the American Indian that have been perpetuated by Hollywood. He lays particular stress on the historical antecedents for the stereotypes adopted by the movies that demonstrated the cultural heritage of such misconceptions. The images of the Native Americans found in films offer a sharp contrast to the images traditionally held by the Indian of himself. Through literature, film, and textbooks, White culture has consistently distorted, both intentionally and unintentionally, the image of the Native American.

My parents told me that what the movies and history books said about the Indians wasn't necessarily so. This was the greatest gift they could have given me.
— *Buffy Sainte-Marie, Cree*

When the Western Europeans first came to this continent they were faced with a dual problem: first, what to do with the wilderness, and second, what to do with those who inhabited that wilderness. Those early Renaissance Englishmen inherited not only what they believed to be an uncivilized environment but uncivilized people as well. Their task, and they felt it keenly, was to subdue the wilderness and to bring order to this newly found chaos. They wanted to create a civilized Anglo-Saxon society much like the one they had just left, because in such a society human beings could achieve their highest potential. One of the impediments to this progress was "uncivilized man," so these early colonialists set about to civilize the savage American. In the end, the Native American was all but destroyed.

Initially the impulses of the White invaders, however finally disastrous, were at least well intentioned. They wanted to Christianize the Indians into part of their social order. But the Native Americans were not easily assimilated. As Roy Harvey Pearce has pointed out in his seminal study *Savagism and Civilization: A Study of the Indian and the American Mind*,[1] by the end of the 1770s the American Revolution demanded a commitment on the part of the colonials to a new world vision of a glorious civilization, one in which the Indian could play no part. The original notion of the noble savage, a product of what Pearce calls Anglo-French primitivistic thinking, gave way to the realization that the Native American was bound inexorably to "a primitive past, a primitive society, and a primitive environment, to be destroyed by God, Nature, and Progress to make way for Civilized man."[2] Pearce notes that first the colonialists tried to understand the savage and to bring him into civilization; after the dawning of the Republic, the savage became an obstacle in the path of progress.

The transition in mental attitudes from assimilation to annihilation was not an abrupt one and its various permutations need not concern us here. The point is that by the beginning of the nineteenth century there was public recognition of both the failure in theory and in practice of the White man's attitude toward the Indian. Since the Red man would not conform to the way of life of the new society, since he could not or would not be civilized, then he must be destroyed. As Pearce writes, the Whites could pity the Indian and still censure him for his failure to adapt, and in the end this pity and censure would be the "price Americans would have to pay for destroying the Indian, . . . the price of the progress of civilization over savagism."[3]

Despite the wanton destruction of the native environment and of the native cultures, the civilized American remained fascinated by what he regarded as savagism. The Native American was no longer a threat to White expansionism, and by the nineteenth century he formed a curious object for study. The new society of which Americans felt themselves a part craved the assurances of progress and superiority — the Indian became the obvious point of comparison. The Europeans who settled this continent brought with them all the trappings of Western culture, including its needs to know the past and the future. The Native American's "Historyless antiquity," as Leslie Fiedler calls it, was beyond their comprehension.[4] The Indians had no past and no future in Western terms and thereby fell out of society and out of history.

The primitive life, however, was not all bad. From Rousseau, Europeans had learned about the inherent goodness of natural man and the simple life. And Americans inherited the noble savage as part of their literary tradition. But as they began to create their own literature they were forced to modify the noble savage to fit with the preexisting image of the Indian in America — one to be pitied and censured. So the doomed noble savage became a part of American literature. It was easy enough to pity the Indian, especially after his fall from grace, but it was necessary to undercut his nobility as well. One could not wipe out a race of noble men without justification. So writers created the bloodthirsty noble savage. Writers were also forced to admit, albeit hesitantly, the White man's guilt as well as hatred for the Red man. Hatred and guilt mixed with celebration; this view of the noble savage was peculiarly American. The Indian was reduced to a set of contradictions: noble and ignoble, pitied and praised, censured and celebrated. In such a way Americans justified and bolstered their own barbarism. White Americans could become savage, too, in order to crush savagism to save civilization. By the end of the nineteenth century, civilization's victory over savagism was complete.

This view of the ignoble, noble savage has remained with us ever since and only now is beginning to change. Once the Indian had been effectively controlled as a cultural threat he passed into the popular mind of the nineteenth century to emerge full blown and recreated in the Beadle dime novels of the 1860s. The image of the bloodthirsty savage filled the pages of these pulp thrillers. The lurid cover illustrations especially added to this image by often portraying Indians, tomahawks in hand, menacing a blond heroine. The enormous success of Buffalo Bill as a pulp fiction hero helped to seal the fate of the Indian. In these penny dreadfuls the "red varmits" were killed or subdued in the name of morality, nationalism, and patriotism. Practically all the stereotyped Indian clichés that later appeared in films were invented by the pulp fiction writers. In fact, by 1912 some of the later dime novels were actually being adapted to the movies.

Not only was Buffalo Bill possibly the most popular of the dime novel heroes but he was also an extremely successful showman and his wild west show toured all over the world. His show even had a crown performance before Queen Victoria. She was, presumably, amused. Included among the exhibits in the show were real live Indians whom Buffalo Bill paraded around the audience and used in the mock battle scenes he staged between the White settlers and the savages. By the time Buffalo Bill was through, the Indians were firmly established as figures of entertainment like the stage Irishman and the comic Jew.

Since the Indian had high entertainment value, it seemed only natural that Edison should have shot film vignettes of Indian dances for his early penny arcade peep shows.[5] Edison's machines showed such films as the *Sioux Ghost Dance* (1894) and the *Parade of Buffalo Bill's Wild West* (1898). As Ralph and Natasha Friar put it in their book *The Only*

Good Indian . . . : The Hollywood Gospel: "The filmic cultural genocide of the Native American begins with such commercialization as *Sioux Ghost Dance*."[6] There is no historical evidence that what was filmed was the Ghost Dance but filmmakers, always eager to take advantage of ready-made publicity, were probably relying on the public to remember Wounded Knee only four years before. From those earliest dim flickerings of the motion picture, there began the process of miscreating the Native American's culture and way of life. What followed for the next few years was a conscious reworking of history through the re-creation of the battles of the Indian Wars on the silver screen. Audiences were treated to a series of films that touted the mythical, often falsified, exploits of such legendary frontier figures as Kit Carson and Daniel Boone, plus a number of cowboys, including the ever-present Buffalo Bill Cody. The White heroes got the billing, and the Indians got the pratfalls.

D. W. Griffith, Thomas Ince, Cecil B. DeMille, all of the greatest of the early filmmakers, contributed to this stereotype. Yet despite truly talented directors concerning themselves with making films about Indians, the image of the Native American did not become any clearer or more historically accurate. One still saw Sioux-bonneted actors selling Navajo blankets. Even actor-writer-director William S. Hart, who prided himself on the authenticity of his westerns, spewed forth bilge about the White man's supremacy over the Indians in such films as *The Aryan* (1916). One title of this epic read: "Oft written in letters of blood, deep carved in the face of destiny, that all men may read, runs the code of the Aryan race: 'Our women shall be guarded.'"[7] The threat of miscegenation was powerful.

By the time of World War I the image of the Native American was well established in the popular film, and for the next three decades, with some minor exceptions, that image remained constant. The moviemakers expressed the same ambivalence toward the Indian that the dime novelist had. The ignoble, noble savage was still with us. There was one major difference though; because of the visual nature of the new medium, Hollywood had more opportunity to distort our view of the Native American. The writers of pulp fiction sketched in the settings and described the "Red men," but Hollywood actually showed them. The resulting confusion was symptomatic of the White man's ignorance of the people he had dispossessed. Indians of the

Northeast were shown wearing clothing of the Plains Indians and living in dwellings of tribes of the Southwest. Hollywood created the instant Indian: wig, war bonnet, breechclout, moccasins, Hong Kong plastic beadwork. The movie producers did what thousands of years of social evolution could not do, even what the threat of the encroaching White man could not do — Hollywood produced the homogenized Native American, devoid of tribal characteristics or regional differences. As long as an actor wore fringed pants and spoke with a halting accent he was an Indian.[8]

Through the years filmmakers have made little attempt to portray the Native American with historical accuracy. It has been more important to perpetuate the image of the Indian that accorded with the popular myth. One of the things Hollywood has done well is to adapt a popular mythology to the screen, rework it, and give it back to the populace. This reinforcing of stereotypes made a lot of money and the main reason Hollywood existed was to make money. Thus popular films of the last seventy years have represented the Native American as an entertaining anachronism. In spite of the sympathetic representations of Indians by photographers such as Edward Curtis and the White culture's long tradition of scientific curiosity about the Indian, it has been this distorted popular image that has dominated.

Within the last ten years it has become increasingly difficult for Hollywood to maintain the kinds of stereotypes it has been surviving on for years. Films must begin to treat not only Native Americans but women and Blacks as well in some way other than through the distortions produced in the past. As a result, at the moment Indians are disappearing from popular films. Since the moviemakers do not have anything concrete to go on — a clear notion of how an Indian should be portrayed — they are merely excluding them. Where Hollywood studios go from here is anyone's guess; they probably do not have any idea themselves. They have detected a changing image and they are baffled by it. This kind of scrutiny has made the old filmmakers not only self-conscious but wary of moving too fast. For example, even the few attempts to create a more historically accurate picture of the Indian in such films as *A Man Called Horse* or *Little Big Man* have met with varying degrees of success. Directors are still having trouble matching the right Indians with the right locale and in the right stories. Mandan lodges are still appearing in Sioux camp circles. The problems are enormous and filmmakers, for the present at least, have stopped trying to make the accommodations.[9]

What will happen to the image of the Indian in film in the future is impossible to predict. If past history is any guide, films will find or develop a new stereotype, one that will accommodate a new popular image. Mass arts tend to the allegorical, preferring surfaces and types to essences and individuals, which allows them a broader or more universal appeal. And while we can expect to see Native Americans portrayed more sympathetically and with greater historical accuracy, the Indian in the popular film nevertheless will remain as one-dimensional as all stercotypcs.

The cultural distortions perpetuated by the motion picture industry reflect the moral obtuseness and ethical myopia technologically advanced peoples have generally exhibited toward those less advanced. After all, it was the early Greeks, the most civilized of Western cultures, who coined the word barbarian for those peoples who could not speak Greek and were therefore presumably denied access to the Greek way of life. So, too, the English tramped around the globe bearing their White man's burden with admirable tenacity, despite the reluctance of many of the peoples they conquered. It is not surprising then that White Americans allowed their sense of superiority and their allegiance to the idea of a manifest destiny to blunt their sensitivity. Unfortunately, films and television have not done much in the last few years to correct the misperceptions that were created. It would suggest an enormous insensitivity on the part of our culture to continue to produce films in the old way. A reassessment is now in order.[10]

NOTES

1. Roy Harvey Pearce, *Savagism and Civilization: A Study of the Indian and the American Mind* (Baltimore, Maryland: Johns Hopkins University Press, 1965).

2. Ibid., p. 4.

3. Ibid., p. 53.

4. *The Return of the Vanishing American* (New York: Stein and Day, 1969).

5. Most of the following information about the images of Indians found in early films was gleaned from Ralph and Natasha Friar's excellent book *The Only Good Indian . . . : The Hollywood Gospel* (New York: Drama Book Specialists, 1972).

6. Ibid., p. 70.

7. Ibid., p. 137.

8. For a further discussion of this idea see John C. Ewers, *The Emergence of the Plains Indian as the Symbol of the North American Indian* (Washington, D.C.: The Smithsonian Institution, 1964) and the same author's "The Static Images," *Look to the Mountaintop* (San Jose, Calif.: Gousha Publications, 1972), pp. 107–9.

9. For a lengthy and comprehensive discussion of these images see Charles L. P. Silet and Gretchen M. Bataille, "The Indian in the Film: A Critical Survey," *The Quarterly Review of Film Studies* 2 (Feb. 1977): 56–74.

10. For a comprehensive annotated checklist of books and articles on Indians in the film, see Gretchen M. Bataille and Charles L. P. Silet, "A Checklist of Published Materials on Popular Images of the Indians in the American Film," *The Journal of Popular Film* 5 (1976): 171–82.

3 The Unknown Past

Sources for History Education and the Indians of Iowa

L . E D W A R D   P U R C E L L

Problems relating to the interpretation of nineteenth- and twentieth-century Indians in Iowa are dealt with in the following chapter. This study is based on an intensive analysis of ten Iowa history textbooks used extensively in the public school system throughout the state. For the most part these books were found to be replete with inaccurate information and racist or ethnocentric perspectives pertaining to Indians. Here the author explores the sources and impacts of these attitudes from the standpoint of a Euro-American scholar trained in the methods of history. His perspective thus dovetails, but differs from, those presented by Mesquakie writers Bertha Waseskuk and Donald Wanatee, whose chapters appear subsequently in this volume.

Most American history has been written as if history were a function of white culture — in spite of the fact that well into the nineteenth century the Indians were one of the principal determinants of historical events. . . . American histories have made shockingly little effort to understand the life, the societies, the cultures, the thinking, and the feeling of the Indians, and disastrously little effort to understand how all these affected white men and their societies.
— Bernard DeVoto, introduction to Strange Empire *by Joseph K. Howard (1952)*

Indian history is one of Iowa's neglected stepchildren. This is unfortunate, since the tale of Iowa's Indian people is interesting, instructive, and often inspiring. The neglect of Indian history is a matter of special regret in the case of education since much of what is called "social consciousness" depends on understanding history. The issues firing today's movement for Indian rights are based on a knowledge of the past. Leaders of the Indian rights movement refer often to the history of White-Indian relations: to treaties, to dispossession, to historical rights. A clear understanding of the facts of history is vital to those interested in reform or reparation.

This chapter, first published in *The Indian Historian*, Summer 1976, vol. 9, no. 3, appears here in edited form by permission of © *The Indian Historian*.

Major obstacles to understanding the present-day situation are the images and attitudes that non-Indians in Iowa — as elsewhere — have of Indian people. Far too often these images are based on error. Sometimes the error is unwitting, the fault of ignorance rather than malice, yet the results are the same no matter what the intention. Many non-Indian Iowans hold stereotyped views of Indians, usually derived from popular image makers such as television and the movies. The stereotype shows all Indians as nomads of the Great Plains, given to violence and bloodshed, romantic savages now unable to cope with modern civilization.

These images are everywhere and are especially irritating in Iowa where there is little relationship between myth and reality. False images abound nevertheless, such as the use of an "Indian" logo by a bank in Tama, Iowa — the person depicted as the bank's advertising symbol is a Plains tribesman, perhaps a Cheyenne or Sioux, but certainly not an Indian from near Tama.

More irritating than the skewed images reflected from the television screen or neon advertising signs is the equally error-filled information dispensed in the public schools under the guise of history. In Iowa, the history of the state is by law taught in the fifth grade (although many school systems postpone the course until junior high or high school), and Indian history is included in the units on general state history. These classes are often the only major formal contact children have with the history of Indian tribes associated with Iowa. The lessons affect both non-Indian and Indian children. They affect everyone exposed to the public school system: in essence, almost everyone in the state. All the authority of the educational system is behind these lessons.

What, then, is the nature of public school education in Iowa as it touches the history of the Indians who have lived here? A review of ten standard school texts, all designed for classroom use, reveals two general tendencies that are disturbing: (1) all Indians who ever inhabited Iowa are lumped together into an amorphous mass and (2) isolated episodes of violence are overemphasized.[1]

The first tendency is not unique to Iowa school history texts. Almost all material intended for a popular audience displays this fault. In the case of the Iowa school texts, the better books list the tribes, with an occasional attempt to separate them on the basis of language groups such as Algonquian or Siouan. There is seldom any attempt to distinguish differing customs, social organizations, geographic preferences, or any other index of differences.[2]

Often, school texts attempt a romantic or colorful description of Indians in general. This is evidently thought to be more interesting than clear explanation. In most instances this generalized description reinforces factual errors or cultural stereotypes. For example, Margaret Posten in her book *This Is the Place — Iowa* includes the following statement: "The Indians were a superstitious people, afraid to kill a snake because they didn't want to offend it. . . . They also had superstitions about bright stars and comets, and tried to explain many of nature's events with stories and legends."[3] Apparently Posten regards Indian beliefs as superstition, but other stories and legends about bright stars — such as the Christian Christmas story of following the star to Bethlehem — are to be taken as valid. Posten fails to note that one person's superstition may be another's religion. Further examples abound in this text, such as the author's description of wickiups as "crude quonset huts."[4] I submit that exactly the opposite is true: the quonset hut is a crude attempt by a technological society to duplicate a simple, cheap, and efficient design, the result being relatively expensive and not nearly so habitable.

The second general tendency of school texts is a bias toward violent episodes in the past. Two events are always discussed: the Black Hawk War and the so-called Spirit Lake Massacre. The series of encounters in 1832 between Black Hawk's Sauk band and White troops, scarcely deserving to be called a "war," did not even take place in Iowa. The entire affair was conducted on the Illinois side of the Mississippi River over contested land in Illinois. Of course the consequences of the war — the forced sale of Iowa lands by the Sauks and the Mesquakies — did pertain to this state. However, to make this episode a major part of textbook Iowa history is silly.[5]

The killing of White settlers in 1857 by a band of dissident Sioux near Spirit Lake is another matter. There is no denying that this event was a part of Iowa's past, but the textbooks dwell on the massacre in bloody-minded detail and at unreasonable length. There is usually an extreme emphasis on the violence, almost as if it were necessary for pioneer Iowa to live up to the latter-day image of the western movie. Given the impressionable nature of grade school children, this treatment probably has a lasting effect. It may be that children remember little else about Indians in Iowa history. Worse, perhaps, than the overemphasis is the garbled way the massacre is presented. A few of the textbook authors do note that the leader of the dissident band, Ink-pa-du-ta, had some provocation: a starving winter, the murder of another Sioux leader by a White man, and exclusion from the 1851 treaty. Yet, in every case, other facts are wrong. All the texts miss the point that the settlers had no business being so far in advance of White settlement.[6]

Perhaps the most significant story of Indians in Iowa history is either missing altogether from the textbooks or very badly confused. One of the most prominent tribes in Iowa's past has been the Mesquakies. However, little is said in most texts about this tribe, and if they are mentioned errors usually predominate. A quick sketch of the history of the Mesquakies will indicate the historical significance of these omissions.[7] The Mesquakies (or Fox as many Whites have called them) migrated to Iowa late in the eighteenth century. They were at that time closely allied to the Sauks, their close cousins in language and social customs. The Mesquakies had fought a long and nearly disastrous series of wars with the French in Wisconsin before they moved into what was to become Iowa. The tribe was noted for independence and fierce resistance to French encroachments on the northern fur trade. Settling primarily on the western side of the Mississippi along several river valleys and near the lead mines at Dubuque, the tribe evidently concluded that the time for fighting Whites had passed, since they maintained peaceful relations with the Americans who assumed interest in the region after the Louisiana Purchase in 1803.

The government of the United States began immediately to misunderstand and mistreat the Mesquakies. In 1804 under dubious circumstances a treaty was signed which established relations between the United States and a tribe designated as the "Sauk and Fox." Despite the fact that a later treaty was signed in 1815 with the "Fox" alone, the federal government has persisted in regarding the two tribes as one. Although at times confederated, the Mesquakies and Sauks were growing further apart during the early nineteenth century.

Because the government insisted on viewing the two tribes as one, the punitive treaty following Black Hawk's defeat in 1832 forced the sale of land by the Mesquakies even though they had not been involved in any of the fighting in Illinois. The tide of White settlement, of course, continued to roll over Iowa, and a further series of treaties finally dispossessed the Mesquakies of all land by the mid-1840s. In 1846 they, along with the Sauks, were removed to Kansas. Many family hunting groups eluded the government, however, and remained in the state. By the 1850s the portion of the tribe in Kansas was completely dissatisfied with conditions there (including bad water, typhus, and lack of game) and concluded on a policy of returning to Iowa. Following a plan devised by tribal leaders, the Mesquakie sought and received permission from the Iowa General Assembly in 1856 to buy and live on land in the state.

This was brilliant strategy. The Mesquakies turned the institutions of White civilization to their own use. By purchasing and holding title to land, they were able to avoid many of the destructive federal Indian policies of the late nineteenth and early twentieth centuries. Because the lands were private property the Mesquakies were able to construct a cultural and ethnic enclave in the heart of White, agricultural Iowa. As a result, they preserved to a remarkable degree the integrity of their native cultural, political, and social institutions.

It is important to note the historical significance of the support offered to the tribe by the state legislature both initially in 1856 and throughout the rest of the 1800s. The close involvement of the governors of the state and their advocacy of Mesquakie rights vis à vis the Office of Indian Affairs (which continued to insist that the Mesquakies belonged in Kansas or, later, Oklahoma) was a major event in Iowa history and highly unusual in the history of White-Indian relationships in America. The picture that emerges from the history of the Mesquakies in Iowa in the nineteenth century is one of a highly intelligent people, working nonviolently to preserve or recover their rights and their way of life, refusing co-optation but skillfully using White allies. The close cooperation between state government and tribe flies in the face of historical generalities. *This* is the major story of Indians in Iowa history during the 1800s, not the aberrant incidents of the Black Hawk War and Spirit Lake Massacre.

Turning to the grade school Iowa history textbooks, one finds the story of the Mesquakies is almost always absent, and if included, it is usually reported incorrectly. The most recent grade school text considered was William Houlette's 1970 *Iowa the Pioneer Heritage*. Houlette does take note of the separate identities of the Sauks and Mesquakies, even though he refers to the latter tribe as the Fox. As to the history of the tribe after 1846, however, he devotes a total of two paragraphs. Rather typically, the text goes on at great length about Black Hawk and Keokuk and the 1832 War.[8]

Bernice Reida and Ann Irwin in *Hawkeye Adventures*, published in 1966, are better at getting the facts straight than most of the textbook authors, but their statements about Indians are replete with invidious cultural comparisons. Consider the assumptions contained in the following statement: "The Sac and Fox of the Woodland culture were, perhaps, the most advanced of any Indian tribes living in Iowa. Some historians believe they were on the verge of making a great step toward civilization when the white man came."[9] The authors do not go on to explain the consequences of the arrival of Whites on the Indians' great leap forward. They share the usual textbook interest in the Black Hawk War and the Spirit Lake business, devoting fifteen pages of text to Spirit Lake, but failing to mention the history of the Mesquakies after 1846.[10]

Margaret Posten in her previously discussed book tells the story of the Mesquakies in four and one-half pages. The basic structure of her explanation is reasonably accurate, but the details are badly confused. For example, she says: "In 1857, three chiefs came from Kansas with money they had saved. . . ."[11] The year actually was 1856, and the three were not all "chiefs," although White writers have tended in general to regard any Indian whom they could for some reason distinguish from the mass of Indians (by name, for example) as a "chief." More garbled is Posten's statement: ". . . even though the Indians living in Iowa today are really of the Fox tribe, they are called Mesquakies."[12] In truth, the name "Mesquakie" translates into English roughly as "red earth people" and is the name the tribe has for itself. In the seventeenth century, a group of Mesquakies of the Fox clan met French trader-explorers. When asked who they were, the Mesquakies replied with the name of their clan. The French attached the label "Renard" to the entire tribe, which was later translated as "Fox," If there is any real name for the tribe it must be the one they use themselves — "Mesquakie."

Another point of error, although admittedly a tricky one, appears in her statement: "The Tama reservation was established for them [the Mesquakies] in 1896."[13] There never has been a reservation for the Mesquakies in Tama County. The tribe lives on a settlement, which was purchased legally from private owners and which is not government property. The often-heard claim that the land is a reservation causes justifiable irritation among the tribe. Posten's confusion here probably springs from a complex series of events that took place in the late 1890s. Since 1856 the state of Iowa had assumed legal responsibility for the tribe. In the nineties, however, a group of Whites in Tama and Toledo, Iowa, acting in the spirit of the Helen Hunt Jackson reformers, took steps to "save" and "civilize" the tribe. One move was to lobby both in Washington, D.C., and Des Moines for the transfer of responsibility from the state to the federal government. In 1896 the General Assembly of Iowa passed a law relinquishing any responsibility in favor of the federal authorities. This did not establish a reservation, since the land was never in question during all of this.[14] Posten's difficulties with this point may be excused since several generations of government officials and attorneys have struggled with the same issue.

Little such allowance can be made for Don Doyle Brown, author of *Iowa, The Land across the River*, published in 1963 (a shorter version entitled *Tell a Tale of Iowa* was published in 1965). Brown's text, one of the most widely used in the state, fails to mention the Mesquakies at all. He does have a full, lengthy, and particularly offensive account of the Spirit Lake Massacre.[15] Hubert Moeller's *Hawkeye Tales*, published first in 1953, carries almost the same treatment — nothing about the Mesquakies after 1846 but a full report of the Spirit Lake affair.[16]

One of the more objectionable texts is *Iowa Beautiful Land*, written by Jessie Dwelle in the early 1950s. It is probably sufficient to merely quote two of her chapter titles: "Indians Have Mirth" and "No Domestic Government in the Indian Home." Dwelle also provided the following caption for a picture of a young woman in a Hollywood Indian costume: "Indian maidens were often found to be very beautiful and fond of gaudy display in dress and ornaments." Of course, there is nothing in this text about the post-1846 history of the Mesquakies, and six pages are devoted to the Black Hawk War.[17]

Of all the school texts normally in use in Iowa grade school classes only one has an accurate and balanced account of Mesquakie history. Herbert V. Hake's *Iowa Inside Out*, published in 1968, is the sole book to state clearly the sequence of events in the mid-nineteenth century that led to the establishment of the Mesquakie Settlement. Hake devotes several pages to the Mesquakie story after 1846, gets their tribal name correct, and makes a point of explaining the purchase of tribal land.[18] While it is cheering to find at least one example of accuracy and balance among the texts, the overall odds of nine to one are a bit depressing.

The generally low quality of Iowa school texts, at least as they touch on Indian history, must be abundantly clear by now. The questions raised from this survey of standard teaching materials are why are they so bad and why do they contain so many errors of fact and interpretation? Thinking about the chronological sequence of the publishing dates of the texts begins to provide some answers. It becomes clear that the latest text writers have relied heavily on the work of their predecessors. The textbooks of the 1960s and 1970s owe a major debt to the textbooks of an earlier day. In many cases the later books do little more than paraphrase earlier works. This is, of course, to be expected. The writers of texts are almost never specialists in history and seldom if ever conduct their own research into original sources. It would be absurd to expect them to do so. The textbook writers (and the classroom teachers as well) must rely on what is readily available to them. The fault, then, may rest with the easily available sources.

The most frequently used sources seem to be those from the pen of a very distinguished Iowa historian, Ruth Gallaher, who was for many years on the staff of the State Historical Society of Iowa. Her first published work on Iowa Indian history was in 1905. In later years she popularized the story of the Mesquakies in an article in the February 1936 issue of *The Palimpsest*.[19] This article on the "Tama Indians" is perhaps one of the most readily available sources on the Mesquakies, since it has been reprinted at least three times. Gallaher also published a school text in 1929 entitled *Stories of Iowa for Boys and Girls* in collaboration with another member of the Historical Society staff, Bruce Mahan. All in all this book is probably the best researched and written Iowa grade school history text in existence. It does, however, have faults. While the main outlines of the Mesquakie story are correct, subtle slanting of emphasis makes both the 1929 text and the earlier *Palimpsest* article difficult to use as sources for textbook writing. Only very careful reading and some degree of independent knowledge allow proper use of these materials as a base upon which to build further texts. After reading Gallaher's work, it is not difficult to understand how later authors began to confuse and garble the history of the Mesquakies. Gallaher's insistence on using "Tama Indians"—thus interjecting yet a third name for the tribe — is by itself ground for confusion.

Unquestionably the most upsetting example of repeated error is found in a study guide prepared for use in the Iowa City school system. This purely local material contains the worst example of blanket cultural defamation I have ever seen in regard to the Indians of Iowa. The characterizations of the Mesquakies in this study guide are not only libelous but entirely unfounded. To quote:

> Though the Sauks and Foxes were neighbors, and most of the time friends, they were not exactly alike. The Sauks listened to good advice; they thought twice before they raised the war whoop; they usually traded fairly; and they kept their word. But the Foxes were every man for himself. Many of them were so greedy that they were willing to cheat and steal. In spite of their bad character they were very religious.[20]

This statement, which can only be described as totally false, is dumbfounding. It is also nearly opposite of the truth. the Sauks were far and away the more warlike of the two tribes, at least within the time period of contact with Americans. The Mesquakie almost never fought Americans and avoided complicity with Black Hawk both in 1815 and 1832. The incredible statements about greed, cheating, unreliability, and all the rest are so much hogwash. This study guide would be laughable, until it is remembered that public school children learn this as history.

I was most perplexed about this study guide when I attempted to discover the motivation for such statements. I could hardly believe that the two local teachers credited with putting together the guide could harbor such a grudge against the Mesquakies. In fact, I rather doubted that the two teachers had ever met a member of the tribe.

Following sources backward in time, the mystery was soon clarified. The Iowa City study guide is an almost exact quotation from a text published in 1939 by yet another employee of the State Historical Society of Iowa, John Ely Briggs. Briggs was the long-time editor of *The Palimpsest* and enjoyed a reputation as a fine historian, especially adept at popularizing history for a wide audience. It is apparent, however, that he had a very strong anti-Mesquakie bias. The tribe was the focus of not only his prejudice but also some very sloppy research.

Many of Briggs's facts are just wrong. Worse, he clearly regarded the Mesquakies of the twentieth century who lived on the Settlement as a degraded remnant of what was once a noble and savage race.[21] It is hard to imagine missing the point of Iowa Indian history more totally. Unfortunately, Briggs was chosen as the source and model for the Iowa City study guide.

At this point it is clear that the earlier generation of textbook writers, who became the models for later authors, were themselves at the mercy of available sources. The major inadequacies of Iowa Indian history begin to emerge clearly. In short, the state's historians have failed miserably to record and interpret the heritage of the Indian in Iowa. There is literally nothing comprehensive or well researched now available on the subject. Thus it is that anyone writing a grade school textbook is faced with an insurmountable problem. There is nowhere to turn, except to previous texts with all their faults. The only alternative would be years of strenuous research into newspapers, government documents, and private papers, obviously an absurd procedure for every topic that must be covered in a school text.

There is only one major work now in existence on the topic of Iowa's Indians. A clergyman, Alexander Fulton, published a book entitled *The Red Men of Iowa* in 1882.[22] Over one hundred years old and written well before most state history had yet occurred, this book is — almost unbelievably — the sole comprehensive history of Iowa's Indians. The deficiencies of the book are legion, although it should be noted that it does have value. Unfortunately, it was authored by a man who, rather typically for the time, viewed the Indians as a dying race, childlike curiosities about whom it would be good to record some idle bits of information before they disappeared from the earth.

Almost all other general histories of the state spring from essentially the same ground. Volumes by Benjamin Gue and Cyrenus Cole, both nineteenth-century newspapermen and politicians, reflect the strengths and weaknesses of their backgrounds.[23] They were not professional or objective historians (nor did they pretend to be), and their work, while useful, is not reliable where it touches on the heritage of the Indian.

Following the story of Indians in Iowa through the most recent school texts, back through earlier texts, and eventually to history books is a depressing and frustrating experience. Even more frustrating is the knowledge that there is no easy cure at hand. The only solution is a renewed interest in Indian topics on the part of the state's historians. Much basic work needs to be done in the sources, and new articles and books need to be written. A massive effort toward clarifying the past must be made before any faults of the texts will be corrected. It would be wise for Iowa's present-day Indian leaders to promote such an effort; until it is undertaken and completed both Indian and non-Indian children will continue to be misinformed and misled. As things now stand Indian history in Iowa is, sadly, "The Unknown Past."

NOTES

1. The ten school textbooks used in this study are: William Houlette, *Iowa the Pioneer Heritage* (Des Moines: Wallace Homestead, 1970); Herbert V. Hake, *Iowa Inside Out* (Ames: Iowa State University Press, 1968); Bernice Reida and Ann Irwin, *Hawkeye Adventure* (Lake Mills, Iowa: Graphic Publishing, 1966); Margaret L. Posten, *This Is the Place — Iowa* (Ames: Iowa State University Press, 1965); Don Doyle Brown, *Tell a Tale of Iowa* (Des Moines: Wallace Homestead, 1965); Allan Carpenter, *Enchantment of America: Iowa* (Chicago: Children's Press, 1964); Jessie M. Dwelle, *Iowa Beautiful Land: A History of Iowa* (Mason City, Iowa: Klipto Looseleaf Co., 1958); Hubert Moeller, *Hawkeye Tales* (Des Moines, Iowa, 1953); John Ely Briggs, *Iowa, Old and New* (New York: University Publishing Co., 1939); and Bruce Mahan and Ruth Gallaher, *Stories of Iowa for Boys and Girls* (New York: Macmillan, 1929). Many of these have been reissued several times in later editions, and *Tell a Tale of Iowa* was originally published in slightly different form as *Iowa, the Land across the River* (1963).

2. Houlette, *Iowa the Pioneer Heritage*, pp. 2–3; Dwelle, *Iowa Beautiful Land*, pp. 8–10; Posten, *This Is the Place*, pp. 115–28.

3. Posten, *This Is the Place*, p. 126.

4. Ibid., p. 119.

5. The only modern history of the Black Hawk War is Cecil Eby, *"That Disgraceful Affair": The Black Hawk War* (New York: W. W. Norton, 1973).

6. The best study of the Spirit Lake episode is still Thomas Teakle, *The Spirit Lake Massacre* (Iowa City: State Historical Society of Iowa, 1918). There are, however, literally hundreds of published articles, reminiscences, and stories on the subject. Most of these are very slanted toward the White, kneejerk side, most notably Abigail Gardner Sharp, *History of the Spirit Lake Massacre* (Des Moines: Iowa Printing Co., 1885. Also reprinted several times since, including 1971 by Wallace Homestead.).

7. Mesquakie history is not assembled in one place but must be pieced together from many published and unpublished sources. Many articles have appeared in periodicals such as *The Iowa Journal of History and Politics* and *The Annals of Iowa*, but much remains to be ferreted out of original sources such as the correspondence and reports of the Office of Indian Affairs. The most recent brief and incomplete survey

of late nineteenth- and early twentieth-century Mesquakie history is L. Edward Purcell, "The Mesquakie Indian Settlement in 1905," *The Palimpsest* 55 (Mar./Apr. 1974): 34–55.

8. Houlette, *Iowa the Pioneer Heritage*, pp. 4–13, 20.

9. Reida and Irwin, *Hawkeye Adventure*, p. 89.

10. Ibid., pp.116–31.

11. Posten, *This Is the Place*, p. 144.

12. Ibid., pp. 144–45.

13. Ibid., p. 145.

14. See Purcell, "Mesquakie Settlement," pp. 41–45; E. C. Ebersole, J. R. Caldwell, and Horace M. Rebok, *History of the Indian Rights Association of Iowa and the Founding of the Indian Training School* (Toledo, Iowa; ca. 1900); and J. R. Caldwell, *A History of Tama County, Iowa*, vol. 1 (Chicago: Lewis Publishing Co., 1910).

15. Brown, *Land across the River*, pp. 99–104.

16. Moeller, *Hawkeye Tales*, pp. 23–43.

17. Dwelle, *Iowa Beautiful Land*, pp. 7–16, 33–58.

18. Hake, *Iowa Inside Out*, pp. 133–38.

19. Ruth Gallaher, "The Tama Indians," *The Palimpsest* 7 (Feb. 1926): 44–53.

20. M. Clatterbaugh and P. Seavy, "A Study Guide to Iowa History" (Iowa City), p. 15.

21. John Ely Briggs, *Iowa, Old and New*, pp. 113–49.

22. Alexander Fulton, *The Red Men of Iowa* (Des Moines: Mills and Co., 1882).

23. Benjamin F. Gue, *History of Iowa*, 4 vols. (New York: Century History Co., 1903); Cyrenus Cole, *A History of the People of Iowa* (Cedar Rapids: Torch Press, 1921).

4 The Native American Experience in Iowa

An Archaeological Perspective

DAVID MAYER GRADWOHL

This chapter reviews Iowa prehistory as it is known through archaeological evidence and endeavors, once again, to extinguish the myth that a lost race of "civilized" cultures once preceded the resident "savage" Indians whom the invading Euro-Americans perceived in the seventeenth and eighteenth centuries.

The White people speak of the country at this period as "a wilderness," as though it was an empty tract without human interest or history. To us Indians it was as clearly defined then as it is today; we knew the boundaries of tribal lands, those of our friends and those of our foes.
—Francis La Flesche, Omaha

I

In the beginning God created the heaven and the earth. Now the earth was unformed and void. . . . And God said: "Let there be light." And there was light. . . . And God said: "Let us make man in our image, after our likeness; and let them have dominion over the fish of the sea, and over the fowl of the air, and over the cattle, and over all the earth."
(*Genesis*, Chapter 1)

I am a Mesquakie — my Creator made me in his own likeness and he made this country for me. My Creator placed me on this earth. . . . I see him in Grandmother Earth who gives me my food, both wild and from the seed I plant; I see him in the sun from whom I receive warmth and health; I see him in the trees around me from whence I get material for shelter, bark and roots for my medicine and wood for my fire; in the rivers and streams he has placed fish and turtle for me; wild game and fowl are always plentiful so that I might have plenty to eat.
(Bertha Waseskuk, *Mesquakie History — As We Know It*)

This land of the great plains is claimed by the Lakotas as their very own. We are of the soil and the soil is of us. We love the birds and beasts that grew with us on this soil. They drank the same water we did and breathed the same air. We are all one in nature. . . . How long the Lakota people lived in these Midwest plains before the coming of the white men is not known in tribal records. But our legends tell us that it was hundreds and perhaps thousands of years ago since the first man sprang from the soil in the midst of these great plains. . . . Up and up the man drew himself until he freed his body from the clinging soil. At last he stood upon the earth . . . the rays of the sun hardened the face of the earth and strengthened the man and he bounded and leaped about, a free and joyous creature. From this man sprang the Lakota nation and, so far as we know, our people have been born and have died on this plain.

(Luther Standing Bear, *Land of the Spotted Eagle*)

History is the today of another age . . . peopled by the you and I of another time . . . living lives not unlike ours on another level of eternity's spiral.

(Lewis C. Debo, *Ottumwa Courier*)

Now it is . . . prewritten history that we mean when we speak of prehistory . . . the study of man's past before he began to record it himself in symbols that can now be read. . . . The material which the prehistorian uses — which he interprets — is by definition, and by fact, unwritten. It is the unwritten remains of the early past of man . . . in a word it is all archaeological material.

(Glyn Daniel, *The Idea of Prehistory*)

II

There are many perspectives and images of the past. These various perceptions of what we have been — and what we think we have been — are important to us today in how we see ourselves and the manner in which we relate to others.

In this chapter I will attempt to present an archaeological perspective and a set of images of the past human experience in what we now call Iowa, "discovered" in 1673 by a French Jesuit priest (Father Jacques Marquette) and a noted explorer-cartographer (Louis Jolliet), "given" statehood in 1846 by the United States Congress and President James Polk, and "named" after one of the many Native American groups, the Siouan-speaking Ioway, who lived for a time in this geographic area. Long before that time other Native Americans had "discovered" and inhabited the land. For the most part we do not know their specific "tribal" affiliations or their individual names as we often know for the Euro-Americans from their written records. Nevertheless much of the Native American experience going back thousands of years can be discerned through archaeological techniques. The archaeological perspective and the resulting images, though unavoidably incomplete, supplement the past as we know it from legends, myths, and written records.

In this chapter I first identify what I see as the nature of the archaeological perspective and its relationship to other perspectives of the past. Next follows a brief critical analysis of the manner in which Euro-American writers often have interpreted the Native American past in Iowa. Then the general sequence of events in Iowa's past is outlined on the basis of the presently available archaeological evidence. The latter set of images will, of course, need to be modified in the future as new evidence is discovered. Yet the general perspective and knowledge of the broad outlines of Iowa's past, I maintain, can contribute to a more meaningful discussion of present group identifications, social responsibilities, and cross-cultural understanding.[1]

III

Each people has images of its past — legends, folk tales, myths, and songs handed down by word of mouth from parent to child, from generation to generation. These images are always rich in metaphors and other figurative allusions and are oftentimes embellished through the years as individuals repeat the story. Together they form a body of literature referred to as oral tradition. In time certain versions of the oral traditions often are written down and become more tangible images of man's past, for example, portions of the Judaeo-Christian *Bible*, Luther Standing Bear's *Land of the Spotted Eagle*, or Bertha Waseskuk's *Mesquakie History — As We Know It*.

History provides another perspective of the past. In constructing their images of past events, historians work primarily with written records: journals, autobiographies, tax lists, census records, and many other documents, including the written versions of oral traditions. In Iowa there are no written documents prior to those of the French in the late seventeenth century A.D. Historians attempting to describe the events in North America between the sixteenth and nineteenth centuries use not only the written records of "history" per se but also the

FIGURE 4.1. *Archaeological investigations at site 13PK149 (Darr-es-Shalom), a Woodland Tradition site located within the permanent conservation pool of Saylorville Reservoir in Polk County, Iowa. Photo courtesy Chuck Anderson,* Des Moines Tribune.

information provided by ethnography, the anthropological description of living groups of people. In recent years anthropologists and historians have refined what has been called "ethnohistory" or the "ethnohistoric approach." Within a comparative or cross-cultural framework, ethnohistorians attempt to reconstruct the cultural and historical backgrounds of particular groups primarily through a critical examination and evaluation of written records.

Still another perspective comes from prehistory — the study of the past back through the many hundreds and thousands of years before writing was developed or introduced into an area. This is the task of archaeology, working back from the "known" data of written records and ethnographic studies into the "unknown" events of the past as they are reflected in the imperfectly preserved remains and contexts of various structures, tools, and other artifacts humans have made. A primary method archaeologists use to interpret past behavior patterns consists of controlled excavations, that is, carefully uncovering and recording the spatial relationships of artifacts to each other (Figures 4.1 and 4.2). The relationships of groups of artifacts through

David Mayer Gradwohl

FIGURE 4.2. *Iowa State University students uncovering a prehistoric archaeological site in Saylorville Reservoir, along the Des Moines River. Note the use of trowels and other small tools in searching for artifacts and other indications of prior human activities at this site. Photo courtesy Jerome Thompson.*

time can often be determined by techniques such as stratigraphy (a study of the different layers of soil) or carbon-14 dating (the laboratory determination of amounts of radioactive carbon in organic substances such as wood and bone). The archaeologist can and does work within the time period of written records, but it is the prehistoric past that is the unique realm of the archaeologist, for it is that part of the human experience that lies beyond the grasp of the historian and the ethnologist. Given the peculiar nature of archaeological evidence, the story archaeologists tell must be considered a set of images no less than those reflected in different oral traditions or varying written accounts.

At first glance it might appear that these various images and perspectives are inescapably separate and even conflicting. Oral traditions are often considered as part of religion and philosophy — the different perceptions various people have of the universe and their relationship to or within that existential system. On the other hand, history, ethnology, and archaeology stem from the "Western" systematic knowledge-seeking system called science. I would argue, however, that the two approaches are quite compatible and supplement each other in our understanding of the past. Bertha Waseskuk and Luther Standing Bear, for example, speak of an intimate system of earth, rocks, trees, and animals within which they and their people have existed since creation. The Native Americans view themselves as integral parts of the earth, the birds, and the animals. It is *from* these kindred beings that they received their shelter, their food, and their medicine. It is *to* these resources that archaeology looks in reconstructing its story of the past: tools chipped from stone; wood used in constructing shelters and building fires; pottery formed from the soil and fired in open hearths; the bones of fish and animals taken as sources of food, clothing, and tools; and the remains of seeds that prehistoric people gathered in the woods and prairies or harvested from gardens planted along the banks of rivers and streams. This evidence, set in a chronological framework, provides the basis for understanding much about the different life-styles human groups have developed through time.

IV

For the most part, the Native Americans of Iowa come off rather poorly when described in general textbooks written by Euro-Americans. The inadequacies, if not blatant racism, of many of these sources are set out in a more systematic fashion by Edward Purcell in Chapter 3. In general it can, I think, be stated that the Native Americans struggling for their homes and land are no more described as epic heroes than are the American colonial revolutionists regarded in glowing terms by English authors. The following excerpts from *High Points in Iowa History* published by Eugene N. Hastie in 1966 reflect the image too often presented to Iowa school children, Indian and White alike:

> The true and primitive Americans were the Indians, who were found in all parts of the United States. There are over 100 different named tribes, and to say that they were all alike would be far from the truth. They all do have many things in common, such as roving and indolence. . . .
>
> The men cared little for work, but spent their time hunting, fishing and trapping. . . .
>
> Being aliens to Christianity they had little to elevate their thoughts and actions. . . .
>
> Sometimes men, women and children would be drunk. They called it "fire water." Between their annual annuities from the government and the money they received from furs they had considerable money for those times, but they used poor judgement in using it. . . .
>
> Dances of various kinds were common, some of which were strenuous and degrading, for they were savages indeed, not knowing the true God. Their god was the Great Spirit, more vague than real, and arrival at the Happy Hunting Ground was their ultimate goal.
>
> The Sioux were the most vicious and caused more trouble than any of the others. Who hasn't heard of the massacre of General Custer's army, by Sitting Bull and his warriors.
>
> The various tribes were friendly except the Fox, who lived along the Wisconsin River. They were so busy in fighting the other tribes that there was little time for the taking of the fur harvest.
>
> Whether our government did right by the Indians is a debatable question. No doubt they were sometimes tricked and coerced into signing away their lands. Yet the government paid them large sums of money over extended periods and tried to teach them better ways, especially in agriculture. If they had kept their lands and retained their ways the whole country would still be as it was when Columbus discovered America.[2]

A critical analysis of Hastie's book would be an extended essay in itself. Suffice it to say that his book, perhaps a bit more ethnocentric than some, generally reflects what the Euro-Americans usually had to say about the Native Americans. In some ways it is not difficult to see where the Euro-Americans were coming from in their philosophy. After all, their God had given them *dominion* over all the earth and its inhabitants. Add to that the mission of Christianity to bring all pagans to the One and True God, the idea of the "White man's burden," and the concept of "manifest destiny," and you have most of the ingredients necessary for a book such as Hastie's.

Euro-American pioneers and subsequent writers in Iowa, of course, did not initiate the concept that the Native Americans were "savages." It is painful but instructive to recall that in the Declaration of Independence the American colonists included the following item in their list of grievances against King George III: "He has excited domestic insurrections amongst us, and has endeavored to bring on the inhabitants of our frontiers, the merciless Indian savages, whose known rule of warfare is an undistinguished destruction of all ages, sexes and conditions. . . ." At the same time one must observe that some British were known to view the American colonists as "cowards" and "rascals" and even "savages," while Native Americans often perceived all the Euro-Americans as something less than human.

What is true for Euro-American perceptions of the historical or documentary past is even more pronounced in the references to the prehistoric past of the Native Americans in Iowa. They are typically divested of the visible features of their past that are admired by Whites. The conical and effigy mounds, for example, found throughout the state are usually attributed to a lost race of Mound Builders who are supposed to have been more advanced and civilized than the "savages" seen by the first Europeans in the area. Several excerpts from *Hawkeye Tales* published by Hubert L. Moeller (a former superintendent of schools in Palmer, Iowa) in 1963 reflect this line of thinking:

> The first people we have proof of living in Iowa are the "mound builders." We call them this because they built many mounds. Indians that were living in Iowa when white men first reached Iowa also built mounds. It is easy to tell the difference between mounds built by Indians and the mounds built by these ancient people we call "mound builders."

Some people believe the "mound builders" to have been a tribe of Indians. Other people believe they were an entirely different race. We do know that the people that built these mounds were different from any Indian tribes that were found by white men in or near Iowa. . . .

The Mound Builders built roads and cut down many trees. They must have lived in Iowa for several hundred years. We believe that they were an industrious people and at least partly civilized.

What happened to the Mound Builders? No one knows. Perhaps the more savage Indians, who came later, killed all of them. Perhaps the Indians drove them away. They may have moved to the south-west and became [sic] the cliff-dwellers.

The Mound Builders were metal workers. They wove cloth. They were skilled stone workers. The Indians that white men found in Iowa would not do these things. Because of this we believe Iowa's first people, the Mound Builders, were not Indians.[3]

Just to make sure that the school children did not forget the essence of their lesson, Moeller suggested that the following work task be undertaken after the chapter reading was completed: "Make a list of the things the Mound Builders did or made that the Indians did not do or make."

Unfortunately, this viewpoint is not restricted to Moeller's writings. Several additional examples from the books of other authors will perhaps illustrate this point sufficiently. Consider the words of Don D. Brown in his book *Iowa, the Land across the River* published in 1963:

A very primitive people lived in Iowa after the glacial period and historians call these inhabitants Mound Builders because they built mounds for burying their dead.

These Mound Builders were different from Indians but we do not know their exact origin or their race. They disappeared long before the Seventeenth Century and what happened to them is still a mystery. Some believe they were killed by Indians.

This book will deal with Iowa during the years when Indians roamed the fields and woods, and after the Indians the coming of the white man and his struggle to carve out of the wilderness the peaceful and modern state we know today—Iowa, The Beautiful Land.[4]

Here again the image is created of Indians killing off a separate group of mysterious Mound Builders who built the impressive mounds seen throughout Iowa. Furthermore Brown perpetuates the impression of Indians "roaming" around as opposed to the Whites who "struggled" with the wilderness and finally subdued it. The underlying assumption here is, of course, that of "manifest destiny"—the idea that the Euro-Americans were destined to have dominion over the entire Western Hemisphere, the idea that Euro-Americans were entitled to the land because the Native Americans essentially were not "doing" anything with it.

Still another author separates Indians not only from the Mound Builders but from an earlier and even more mysterious group called "prehistoric men." School children reading Jessie M. Dwelle's *Iowa Beautiful Land: A History of Iowa* published in 1958 are told that

the glaciers eventually melted and disappeared. . . . The hills and valleys began to grow trees and flowers and grass, and Iowa became so beautiful that a race of human beings called "prehistoric men" came to this country to live.

Then came the mound-builders. They lived in caves, and they built mounds of earth in which to bury their dead. These people, it is said, were more civilized and soon overpowered the prehistoric men, and the first inhabitants passed from the scene entirely. Next the Indians came, and after that the mound-builders also vanished from this part of the country.[5]

While Dwelle's subsequent discussion of the contact between Native Americans and Euro-Americans is perhaps more objective than that presented by Moeller and Brown, many of the same perspectives and images are still there.

Perhaps one should not be too critical of nonarchaeologists trying to cover Iowa prehistory in more general works concerning the state. But the matter of a "lost race" of "mysterious mound builders" had long been dispelled by the 1950s and 1960s — even in Iowa, via the works of Charles Reuben Keyes going back to at least 1927. In that year Keyes published in the *The Palimpsest* his pioneering synthesis of Iowa archaeology known at that time.[6] A revised version of that article was published in *The Palimpsest* in 1951.[7] Between the 1920s and 1950s Keyes was generally acknowledged as one of the foremost authorities on the archaeology of Iowa. His articles in *The Palimpsest*, a monthly magazine published by the State Historical Society of Iowa, were standard references for professional archaeologists as well as laymen interested in Iowa prehistory. Hubert Moeller, in fact, knew of Keyes's 1927 article as early as 1938 as evidenced in a citation in *Our Iowa: Its Beginnings and Growth*.[8] Even more curious, considering the material quoted above, is Don Brown's reference to Keyes's 1951 article in *Iowa, the Land across the River*.[9] Brown includes the Keyes 1951 article in a list of "teaching references for the prehistoric Iowa period." He further annotates the reference by commenting: "Entire issue should prove very useful."

One wonders if people such as Moeller and Brown really read what Keyes had to say or if they understood the implications of the archaeological evidence. It is difficult for me to comprehend how they could have missed the thrust of Keyes's argument as I reread the 1927 article. Keyes[10] began his discussion as follows:

Myths concerning "vanished races" die very hard. When the pioneers of the white race discovered the great mounds and earthworks of prehistoric man in the Mississippi Valley, they formed the apparently spontaneous judgement that the country had once upon a time been occupied by a race of "mound builders," superior to the painted redskin. In the middle forties of the last century, excavations in the mounds of Ohio which produced finely wrought implements and ornaments of stone, shell, pearl, and copper seemed to be conclusive evidence that predecessors of the Indians had reached a high level of civilization and then vanished before the onslaughts of their savage inferiors.

Surely, thought the pioneer, no wild Indian could ever have constructed the works of such colossal proportions or wrought art objects of such delicacy and beauty. . . . At best it is difficult for one race to understand another and when, after the first friendly greetings, the contest for land engenders hatred and then warfare mutual understanding becomes quite impossible.

But, as the evidence now stands, neither North or South America has any vanished race to record. The American Indian, by every test that it has been possible to apply is the same man who built the great earthworks of the Mississippi Valley, the cliff dwellings and pueblos of the Southwest, the towering temples of Mexico, and the ruined cities of Central America and Peru. The native peoples from Alaska to Patagonia were of one race. Inasmuch as a number of the Indian tribes are known to have built mounds since the coming of the white man, it is quite unnecessary to look farther [sic] for a race of mound builders. When Julien Dubuque died in 1810 he was buried in Iowa soil by his friends, the Fox Indians, who erected a mound over him.

Not only is the lost race of mound builders a fanciful myth, but up to this time there is no proof that the New World ever had a race of men who, in the physical sense, were really primitive.

Keyes's statement was certainly an insightful one for the 1920s — it is no less remarkable in the 1970s. His perspective is still viable and indeed, as outlined in the following portion of this chapter, many of the images he saw in Iowa prehistory still hold up in the light of today's evidence.

The whole story of the Mound Builders is an involved and intriguing one as shown in Robert Silverberg's *Mound Builders of Ancient America: The Archaeology of a Myth* and more recently in R. Clark Mallam's article "The Mound Builders: An American Myth."[11] But enough was known about Iowa archaeology by the 1920s that any subsequent references to prehistoric inhabitants as anything other than Indians must be regarded as insidious if not intentionally derogatory to Native Americans.

V

The archaeological sequence as presently known in Iowa is outlined in Table 4.1. This outline is necessarily of a general nature and uses as its organizing frame the culture-historical periods or traditions that various archaeologists have defined. More extensive discussions of the archaeology of Iowa and particular regions within the state can be found in a number of other sources.[12] The summary here is intended to present the archaeology of Iowa briefly as a series of images reflecting the human experience in this area over the past 12,000 years.

TABLE 4.1 *Generalized Archaeological Sequence in Iowa*

Culture-historical "periods"	Some significant archaeological sites, archaeological complexes, and known ("tribes")	Miscellaneous general comments
LATE HISTORIC	The Bertrand Coalport Kiln & Noah Creek Kiln (MESQUAKIE) Ft. Madison	"Historical archaeology": overlap between history and archaeology; intrusion of Euro-Americans; removal of most Native American groups; establishment of the Mesquakie settlemen.
AD 1800		
EARLY HISTORIC	(OMAHA) & (PONCA) (DAKOTA) (MISSOURI) (IOWAY) (OTO) (ILLINOIS) ("FOX" & SAUK)	Siouan speakers in central and western part of state; influx of Algonquian speakers ("Fox" and Sauk) from east.
AD 1600		
POST-WOODLAND	NEBRASKA CULTURE (Central Plains Tradition) MILL CREEK CULTURE (Middle Missouri Tradition) GREAT OASIS CULTURE (Middle Missouri Tradition?) ONEOTA TRADITION (Possible overlap with Late Woodland groups)	Small to medium-sized villages; economy based on horticulture and hunting; some fortifications; burials usually in flat cemeteries; elaborate pottery with distinctive regional variations. Certain sites within the Oneota Tradition probably represent westward movement of Chiwere Sioux speakers (Ioway-Oto-Missouri group)
AD 1000		
WOODLAND	WOODLAND TRADITION { Effigy Mounds, Hopewellian Mounds & Village Sites, Red Ocher Mounds }	Conical burial mounds — often with elaborate mortuary offerings related to Hopewellian centers in Illinois and Ohio; grit-tempered, cord-impressed pottery; small villages and camp sites; hunting and some incipient cultivation.
500 BC		
ARCHAIC	Turin Site LOGAN CREEK COMPLEX: Simonsen Site, Hill Site, etc.	Hunters of large bison; kill sites and butchering sites; flexed burials at the Turin Site.
6000 BC		
PALEO-INDIAN	CHEROKEE SEWER SITE Surface finds: parallel flaked lanceolate projectile points Surface finds: CLOVIS FLUTED PROJECTILE POINTS (Rummells-Maske Site?)	Lowest level at Cherokee Sewer Site plus surface evidence of big game hunters of the late Pleistocene; probable hunting of mammoths, mastodons and other large now-extinct mammals.
12,000 BC		

As mentioned previously, most of the names given to the archaeological remains representing prehistoric people do not correspond to known "tribal" names; these are beyond the scope of archaeological evidence. It should be noted, however, that the names given to many Native American groups within historic times and still used today are not the designations these people had for themselves. For example, the group whom the French called "Renards" and the British called the "Fox" are people who refer to themselves as the "Mesquakie" or "Red Earth People." Similarly the people known in history as the "Sioux" usually refer to themselves as "Lakota" or "Dakota" or else they employ labels specifying smaller linguistic and/or political groupings — for example, the Santee and Yankton.[13]

The earliest indications we have of prehistoric Native Americans in Iowa consist of stone spear or projectile points of a certain type found occasionally on the surface of plowed fields and in stream beds throughout the state. Spear points of this type, characterized by a flute or channel flake detached from the base of the point, are called "Clovis" projectile points (Figure 4.3A). They are known from many sites in the southern Plains and western United States where they have been found in association with the bones of mammoth, mastodon, and other large mammals that inhabited North America during the so-called Ice Age or Pleistocene. Found in contexts dated at ten to fifteen thousand years old, Clovis projectile points are indicative of what archaeologists call the Paleo-Indian Period or Big Game Hunting Tradition. Here in Iowa these fluted projectile points have not been found yet in direct association with the large Pleistocene mammals or in contexts for which an exact date or time range can be determined. However, at the Rummells-Maske site, a find spot near West Branch, portions of twenty Clovis style projectile points were found in 1965 and 1966.[14] This evidence, along with the surface finds of Clovis projectile points elsewhere in Iowa, suggests that hunters of the early Paleo-Indian Period did inhabit Iowa at least by the time the last glacier was retreating to the north.

Different projectile point forms indicate that other groups of Paleo-Indian Period hunters were in the area prior to a date of approximately 6000 B.C. Various styles of parallel-flaked lanceolate or leaf-shaped projectile points, for example, have been collected as surface finds in Iowa (Figure 4.3B). These projectile point types have been found in areas adjacent to Iowa in contexts associated with the

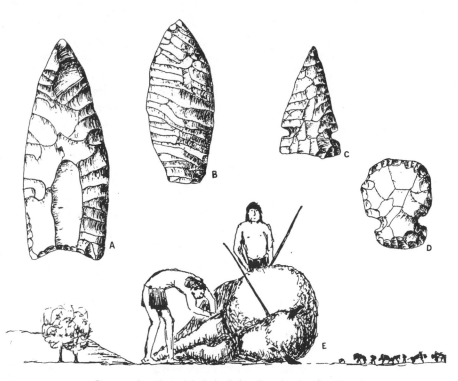

FIGURE 4.3 *Images and artifacts of the Paleo-Indian Period and Archaic Period: (A) Clovis style Paleo-Indian projectile point; (B) parallel-flaked lanceolate projectile point; (C) Logan Creek, Archaic, side-notched projectile point; (D) Logan Creek, side-notched scraper; (E) killing and butchering a large bison.*

large extinct form of bison and dating about 6000 to 8000 B.C. At the Cherokee Sewer Site in northwest Iowa this portion of the Big Game Hunting Tradition may also be evidenced by a lanceolate projectile point found in the lowest of three cultural levels investigated by archaeologists during the summer of 1973.[15] The Cherokee Sewer Site, exposed during the construction of sewage lagoons south of the town of Cherokee, is extremely important to our interpretation of Iowa prehistory because there are three distinct cultural layers stratified one on top of another. This gives a relative time sequence for the three layers in relationship to each other. Furthermore, charcoal samples were collected from these levels and submitted to a laboratory for carbon-14 tests. Carbon from the lowest of the three levels yielded dates of approximately 6500 B.C., which supports the idea that this level represents the Paleo-Indian Period. The two upper cultural layers dated approximately 5000 B.C. and 4000 B.C. The artifacts from these levels plus the carbon-14 dates suggest these occupations at the Cherokee Sewer Site are within the Archaic Period.

By approximately 6000 B.C. the general environment in Iowa had changed considerably. Mammoths, mastodons, and many other large Pleistocene mammals had become extinct in this part of North America. The large species of bison had either become extinct or was being replaced by the modern form of bison. In addition to the two upper levels at the Cherokee Sewer Site, this time period is represented by the Logan Creek Complex known from sites in the Missouri River drainage.[16] Information on this complex, named from the Logan Creek Site in Nebraska, has been excavated at the Simonsen Site and the Hill Site in western Iowa. Carbon-14 dates from sites of the Logan Creek Complex span a period of time roughly 6000 B.C. to 4000 B.C.

The image we have of Native Americans from this time, which archaeologists call the Archaic Period, comes mainly from small camp sites and areas where bison were being killed and processed. In addition to bison these people hunted elk, deer, and smaller mammals. The meat from these animals was prepared as a source of food; their skins and bones were used for clothing and tools. Artifacts used in killing the animals, butchering the meat, and processing the skins include medium-sized side-notched projectile points, side-notched scrapers, plano-convex scrapers and knives of stone, and punches and awls made from bone (Figure 4.3 *C, D, E*). The latter tools may have been used in piercing holes in hides so that they could be sewn together for clothing, containers, and perhaps even shelter covers. The people represented by the Logan Creek Complex also fished and collected freshwater clams in nearby rivers and streams; and they gathered various seeds, nuts, berries, and other wild vegetal resources in the adjoining woods. The plant materials were apparently prepared with grinding stones made from local glacial cobbles. Hearths have been found at most of these Archaic sites although there is little evidence so far as to the type of housing used. A bone whistle found at the Cherokee Sewer Site may represent the earliest musical instrument of this kind known in North America. Whistles and flutes, of course, were used by most Native American groups within the Historic Period.

Somewhat more recent, but still within the Archaic Period, are the skeletons discovered accidentally by a construction worker as he was quarrying in a gravel pit near Turin, Iowa. Here, some twenty feet below the modern ground surface, four individuals had been buried on their sides in flexed positions. At least one individual was covered with red ocher, a pigment made from ground hematite, an iron ore. Associated with these burials were some beads made from shell and one projectile point similar to the Logan Creek style. Carbon-14 dating of organic material from this level at the Turin Site indicates a date of approximately 2700 B.C.

After about 1000 B.C. a new cultural tradition can be identified throughout the eastern United States. It has been called the Woodland Tradition (or Woodland Period) because it appears to represent a series of regional ecological adaptations to the varied woodland environments throughout eastern North America and the westward extensions of the oak-hickory-walnut forest assemblage along the river valleys of the prairies and the eastern Plains. The earliest indications of the Woodland Tradition in Iowa appear about 500 to 200 B.C. Woodland sites are well represented in the period between A.D. 100 and 600, and the tradition continues on to at least A.D. 1000.[17]

During these times Native American groups lived in small communities located along the stream valleys where they continued to hunt and fish and to gather wild plant resources. There were some continuities and some changes in the basic took kits involved in hunting, butchering, and skin working activities. Typical Woodland projectile point forms were corner notched or stemmed (Figure 4.4A). In addition to the hunting and gathering subsistence patterns, there appear to have been initial regional experiments in the growing of corn, squash, sunflowers, and possibly beans. Ground stone axes — typically the "three-quarter grooved" style — were possibly used to clear garden plots (Figure 4.4B). Settlements consisted of small villages of semipermanent dwellings perhaps similar to the bark or mat-covered lodges, resembling Quonset huts in shape, which Euro-Americans observed historically in the Great Lakes region.[18]

Ceramics are an innovation within the Woodland Period (Figure 4.4C, D). Particularly characteristic is the pottery made from clay to which has been added crushed granite or sand. The latter material, a tempering agent, prevents excessive cracking after the pottery vessels are formed and it gives them tensile strength as they are fired in open hearths. Before Woodland pottery was fired, the outside surfaces of the vessels were usually textured by pressing cords of twisted bast fiber

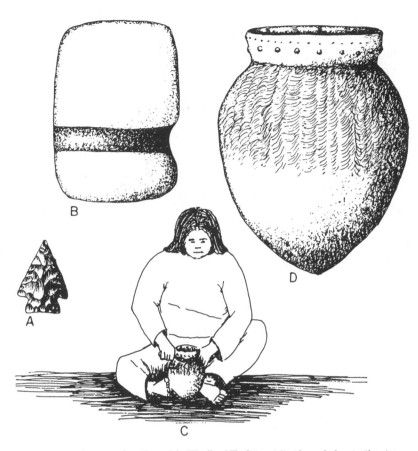

FIGURE 4.4 *Images and artifacts of the Woodland Tradition: (A) side-notched projectile point, (B) three-quarter grooved axe, (C) woman manufacturing a ceramic vessel, (D) Woodland style ceramic vessel.*

into the moist clay. Decorations were often added by punching nodes and by impressing or incising designs below the rims of the pots. Woodland vessels typically lack handles and have elongated conical bases.

Perhaps more familiar indications of the Woodland Period are the conical burial mounds found throughout Iowa and the effigy mounds in the northeastern part of the state. These earthworks appear to represent an elaborate mortuary and ritual complex. As discussed previously these burial mounds are not the works of a mysterious "lost race" but rather a regional Native American burial tradition centering in the Ohio, Illinois, Mississippi, and Missouri river valley systems. Particularly in the conical mounds along the Mississippi valley in Iowa individuals were often interred with mortuary offerings such as shell beads, copper ear spools, carved stone pipes, various tools, and food in ceramic vessels and marine shell containers. In other instances bundles of disarticulated bones were placed in the mounds, perhaps long after the dead person had been left on a wooden platform or scaffold as was the practice of many Plains Indian groups in Historic times.

The burial mound complex along with continuities in pottery and projectile point styles link Woodland communities throughout Iowa with others in Illinois and Ohio. The extensive trade and communications network that existed at this time reached from the Rocky Mountains to the Atlantic coast and from the Gulf coast to the Minnesota/Great Lakes area. In the elaborate Middle Woodland (Hopewellian) mounds in eastern Iowa, Illinois, and Ohio, for example, are sometimes found grizzly bear tooth pendants and tools of obsidian or volcanic glass that ultimately derive from the Rocky Mountains, copper artifacts from sources in the Great Lakes region, marine shell containers and ornaments from the Atlantic and/or Gulf coast, and chert source materials from distant quarries. The rather extensive communication systems (including intertribal trade) that the French and English observed among Native Americans in the eastern United States during the seventeenth and eighteenth centuries no doubt stem back to the Woodland Period to some degree.

After about A.D. 900 or 1000 we see still more changes throughout the prairie-plains regions. In general, settlements appear to increase in size and become more permanent. There seems to be more of an emphasis on horticulture in addition to the continuation of hunting, fishing, and gathering as subsistence activities (Figure 4.5). Typically sites dating from the Post-Woodland Period are characterized by the presence of many cache or storage pits in which garden produce, meats, and tools were stored — in much the same fashion as the later Euro-American pioneers used root cellars. Horticulture is evidenced by remains of the harvested crops (particularly corn, beans, squash, pumpkins, and sunflower seeds) and the tools used in gardening activities — polished stone celts to clear the plots, bone and antler picks and scoops to prepare the soil, and rakes and hoes to cultivate the crops. Bison, elk, deer, and smaller animals were shot with arrows tipped with small triangular projectile points, some with delicate side

FIGURE 4.5 *Images of gardening activities during the Post-Woodland Period:* left, *woman using an antler rake in preparing a garden plot;* right, *woman using a hoe made from a bison shoulder blade.*

and/or basal notches as hafting devices. Meat was removed from the slain animals by a variety of carefully chipped stone knives and scrapers. These tools, along with bone and antler fleshing tools, punches, awls, and needles, were used in the preparation of animal hides and in the production of skin clothing and containers. Human burials in the Post-Woodland complexes tended to be in flat cemeteries rather than the large mortuary mounds. Food, tools, and other items were frequently placed in the grave pits to accompany the dead.

At least four regional variations can be defined in the Post-Woodland Period on the basis of such things as different pottery styles, architectural forms, and settlement patterns. The various pottery styles reflect to some degree separate regional continuities in basic technological traditions and the aesthetic choices made by local groups of women potters over time. Different house structures and settlement patterns may indicate differing kinship and social organizational schemes although that cannot be demonstrated readily from the available evidence.

The Nebraska Culture, located along the Missouri River and its tributaries in western Iowa and eastern Nebraska, is part of the Central Plains Tradition and is characterized by small unfortified villages

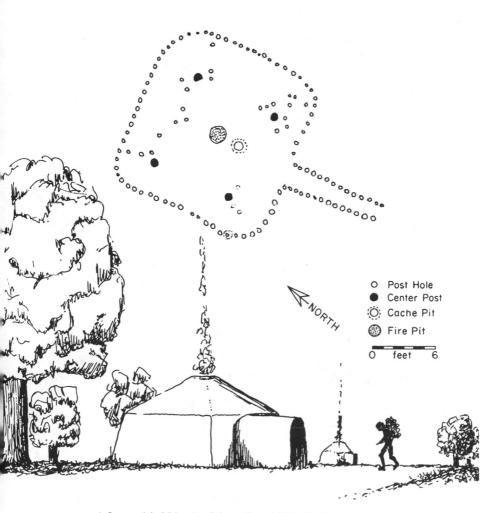

O Post Hole
● Center Post
◎ Cache Pit
⊛ Fire Pit

0   feet   6

FIGURE 4.6 *Images of the Nebraska Culture, Central Plains Tradition:* upper, *excavated floor plan of an earth lodge;* lower, *artist's reconstruction of an earth lodge village.*

of earth lodges that were square in floor plan and had elongated entrance passageways and domelike roofs[19] (Figure 4.6). In basic structure, these early square earth lodges were similar to the historic circular earth lodges of the Mandan and Hidatsa recorded by painters such as Carl Bodmer and George Catlin in the 1830s in what is now North Dakota. William Henry Jackson and other photographers also recorded earth lodges among such groups as the Omaha and Pawnee in Nebraska in the 1870s. The globular Nebraska Culture ceramic ves-

FIGURE 4.7 *Images of Post-Woodland traditions in clay: (A) Nebraska Culture, (B) Mill Creek Culture, (C) Great Oasis Culture, (D) Oneota Tradition.*

sels, quite often with handles, differ markedly from Woodland pottery (Figure 4.7*A*). Vessel rims are most often straight, although some wedge-shaped and S-shaped profiles occur. Decoration, when present, is normally restricted to the lip and the rim exterior. Although the external surfaces of many vessels do exhibit cord-roughened texturing, smoothed surfaces are more frequent on Nebraska Culture pots.

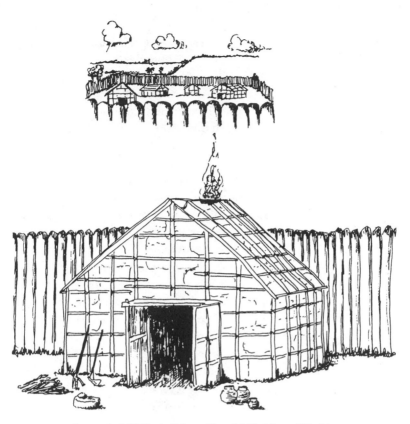

FIGURE 4.8 *Images of a Mill Creek Culture village, Middle Missouri Tradition.*

The Mill Creek Culture, located in northwest Iowa along the Big Sioux and Little Sioux rivers, is considered part of the Middle Missouri Tradition, and is characterized by medium-sized villages that were often fortified with defensive banks and ditches and wooden palisades.[20] The house style consisted of long rectangular structures that probably had gabled roofs (Figure 4.8). Mill Creek pottery, typically globular in shape, usually had rims that were wedge-shaped or S-shaped and decorated in a variety of incised, tool-impressed, and finger-pinched designs. Parallel incised line decoration occurs frequently on the shoulder area of Mill Creek pots (see Figure 4.7*B*).

Another regional variation, the Great Oasis Culture, is also found in northwest Iowa and in central Iowa along the central Des Moines River valley and the lower Raccoon River valley.[21] Named from a type-site in Minnesota, the Great Oasis Culture may represent an eastward extension of the Middle Missouri Tradition. Great Oasis house structures defined in northwest Iowa may be, however, more similar to Nebraska Culture than to Mill Creek architecture. Fortification systems are not demonstrated at Great Oasis sites. Particularly characteristic of this complex is the pottery, usually tempered with fine sand and typically decorated with finely incised decorations on the rim exteriors. As opposed to other ceramic complexes at this time, Great Oasis pottery typically lacks handles (see Figure 4.7C).

A fourth archaeological complex that is seen after A.D. 1000 in Iowa is called Oneota after the presumed aboriginal name for the Upper Iowa River. This complex is usually regarded as centering in the upper Mississippi River valley and then extending westward into the prairies and eastern plains. Sites identified as Oneota are quite numerous in northwest Iowa, northeast Iowa, and along the central Des Moines River valley.[22] Beyond Iowa, Oneota and closely related sites are known from Illinois and Wisconsin to Nebraska and Kansas, and from Missouri to South Dakota and Minnesota. Particularly characteristic of the Oneota Tradition is its pottery, which is tempered with crushed shell and nearly always decorated with intricate variations of line and dot motifs on the shoulder area (see Figure 4.7D). Oneota pots often have elaborate handles. At several sites there is evidence of long oval house structures that were probably covered with bark or woven reed mats (Figure 4.9). At certain Oneota sites in northwest Iowa and northeast Iowa are found glass beads, ornaments of brass, and iron fragments representing knives and kettles. These items bear witness to contacts with European traders and missionaries in the late seventeenth and eighteenth centuries. Archaeologists regard at least some sites within the larger Oneota archaeological complex as the remains of Chiwere-Siouan speaking groups — the Ioway, Oto, and Missouri — on the basis of cartographic, archival, and ethnographic data.[23]

At this time we enter the Early Historic Period, where history and archaeology merge. When the Europeans first came to the Great Lakes area and the upper Mississippi River valley during the seventeenth and early eighteenth centuries, they encountered many different Native American tribes varying in life-styles and political alliances. These people spoke many distinct dialects of several separate language groups. West of the Great Lakes lived speakers of the Algonquian lan-

FIGURE 4.9 *Images of an Oneota Tradition village.*

guages: the Potawatomi, the Sauk, and the Fox or Mesquakie. The Siouan-speaking Winnebago also lived in this region. To the west of the Algonquian groups were speakers of several different Siouan languages. Spreading out from the headwaters of the Mississippi River were bands of the Dakota. Between the Mississippi and Missouri rivers lived the Ioway, Oto, and Missouri Indians. The Omaha-Ponca and Kansa were settled in villages along the Missouri River valley.

In the late eighteenth and early nineteenth centuries, most of the tribes of the Great Lakes area and the northern Mississippi River valley continued generally westward and southward movements due to a combination of several circumstances: increasing encroachment by White settlement, economic factors associated with the fur trade, destruction of game resources as a basis for subsistence, increasing intertribal warfare, and divisive alliances with Euro-Americans. By the late 1700s the Sauk and Mesquakie villages and hunting territories extended from the Mississippi River valley west toward the Des Moines. Generally to the west of these territories were the Ioway, Oto, Missouri, and Omaha. In northeast and northwest Iowa were bands of the Dakota representing groups of the Santee and Yankton.

Soon after the beginning of the nineteenth century, Indians living between the upper Mississippi and Missouri rivers faced the final episodes of what the White man called "manifest destiny." Following battles and skirmishes (such as the Black Hawk War in Illinois) in which the Native Americans were militarily defeated, a series of treaties was negotiated. Between 1830 and 1851, all the Indians living within the present state boundaries of Iowa, including some recently arrived Potawatomi and Winnebago, were forced to cede their lands to the United States government. By 1851 the land cessions were complete. Indian groups were relocated on reservations to the north in Minnesota and to the west in the Dakotas, Nebraska, Kansas, and Oklahoma — that is, with the exception of a small group of Mesquakie who remained in Iowa by hiding out along the Iowa and Cedar rivers. Eventually these Mesquakie arranged, through a White intermediary, to purchase back some of the land they had been forced to cede to the Untied States. In 1856 the Iowa legislature passed a resolution allowing the Mesquakie to remain on those lands in what is now Tama County. Today some 600 Mesquakie live on 3,200 acres of land along the Iowa River — their own settlement, not a reservation.

The story of the nineteenth century is told primarily by historians and anthropologists working with the images left in written records. Archaeology, however, can also contribute to our understanding of the Late Historic Period. Our knowledge of the settlement of this area by Euro-Americans has been supplemented by the archaeological investigation of sites such as military forts (Ft. Madison and Ft. Atkinson); early industrial sites (Coalport Kiln and the Noah Creek Kiln); "lost" towns (Elk Rapids and Coal Valley); the steamship Bertrand, which sank at DeSoto Bend on April 1, 1865; and the President Herbert Hoover birthplace at West Branch. Due to the destruction of archaeological sites by present-day construction activities, it has even been necessary to excavate pioneer cemeteries — for example site 13PK20 (the Henry Woods Site) in Saylorville Reservoir where four individuals were found buried in supine positions in crude wooden coffins. These Euro-Americans, nameless though they lived during the Historic Period, were probably inhumed in the late 1840s or early 1850s. According to the beliefs of their culture they were buried with the heads to the west, facing east, so that on the promised Judgment Day they could rise and face their Creator who, it will be recalled, gave them dominion over all the earth.

VI

In this chapter various images of the past human experience in Iowa have been presented, in particular those of the Native Americans as seen from an archaeological perspective. This experience goes back at least some ten to twelve thousand years. There are many continuities in this experience, in addition to the many changes through time, as seen in the set of images based on the currently available archaeological evidence. These elements of the past have their correlates in the present. Contemporary Native Americans and those known from historical documents share many similar world views and general life-styles while differing a good deal in the languages they speak, the sociopolitical groups within which they organize, and certain specific cultural traditions they observe. Archaeologists can study these continuities and changes and see the Native American past as an interrelated set of experiences leading into the present. The situation is perhaps analogous to the structure of the Euro-American past. The continuity there is often referred to as "western civilization" and is also known from both archival and archaeological sources. Within that entity are the many differences that the Germans, French, English, Catholic Irish, Protestant Irish, and others see among themselves and that anthropologists can also observe from their point of view.

Without romanticizing or embellishing the Native American past, the set of archaeological images includes neither "lost races" of "civilized mound builders" in the prehistoric period nor "primitive savages" in historic times. The builders of the large prehistoric earthworks of North America are no more mysterious or "lost" than the builders of Stonehenge or the walls of Jericho — and this is not to say that we know, or ever will know, all there is to know about these archaeological complexes. Meanwhile we must recognize, without being hypercritical or totally cynical, that the Euro-American past has been guided to some degree by underlying assumptions of God-given rights to dominion over the earth, religious missionary goals, and manifest destiny.

Archaeology not only discovers the achievements of prehistoric times but also provides insights into the processes of culture change still occurring today. At the beginning of this chapter I stated my belief that an archaeological perspective and a knowledge of the broad outlines of Iowa's past could contribute to a more meaningful discussion of present group identifications, social responsibilities, and cross-cultural understanding. This statement is admittedly idealistic though I hope not presumptuous. In his book *The Uses of the Past*, Herbert J. Muller, reflecting on the philosophical perspective of Reinhold Neibuhr, comments that "man is a thinking animal who is 'both the creature and the creator of history,' knowing both necessity and freedom. In his freedom he can and must aspire to better history."[24] This viewpoint, in my opinion, is quite instructive. We can study the past and attempt to understand it from many different perspectives. We can explore the degree to which the past has shaped the present and identify kinds of continuities linking our behavior today with that of yesterday. We cannot, strictly speaking, relive the past again. But we can, perhaps to a larger extent than we are willing to admit, create the present.

In more concrete terms, it seems to me, we can start by recognizing that Native Americans have lived in Iowa for thousands of years. They did not all disappear or "vanish" in spite of the various treaties of the nineteenth century. Native Americans exist in Iowa today. Many Omaha, Winnebago, Dakota, and other Indians live as individuals and families in cities such as Sioux City, Council Bluffs, Des Moines, Waterloo, Cedar Rapids, and Davenport. In a more communal and corporate sense there are the Mesquakie at their settlement in Tama County. These Native Americans, as well as Euro-Americans in Iowa, seek to live in the present with a sense of the relevant past. They cannot recreate the past any more than the Euro-Americans can. But they can continue participating in traditions from the past and they also can revive and reinterpret certain meaningful elements of the past as Euro-Americans are constantly doing.

Native Americans themselves, of course, must decide what kinds of alternative life-styles they wish to follow. But for Native Americans to be able to choose their desired alternatives, the dominant Euro-American society must recognize that many other people do not share, or want to share, its world view and preferred life-styles. Euro-Americans will have to become more sensitized to the consequences of history books that call Native Americans "savages" and divest them of the accomplishments of their past. Euro-Americans will have to better comprehend contemporary cross-cultural factors — for example, the fact that Native American children in public schools come from differing heritages and that the English they speak is often a foreign language they are learning in addition to one or two Indian languages spoken in their homes. Perhaps at that point some of the alternatives sought by Native Americans — for example, bilingual and bicultural schools — will seem more logical and more feasible.

In this sense, better understanding the past, we can face the challenge of creating the present. The stakes are worth considering in terms of what we decide we are and want to be. For the present we live today is tomorrow's past.

NOTES

1. Preliminary drafts of this chapter were submitted to a number of professional colleagues, students, and Native Americans for their comments and criticisms. Those responding included Duane Anderson, Rupert Costo, Hanna Gradwohl, Duane Mackey, Marc Mills, Nancy Osborn, Maria Thomspon Pearson (Running Moccasins), Duane Peter, Richard Watson, Mildred Mott Wedel, and Waldo R. Wedel. While it was impossible to follow all the suggestions offered, many have been incorporated into this version for which I must, of course, assume final responsibility. I deeply appreciate the criticisms received in terms of sharpening my own understanding of the subjects involved and thus, I hope, of being able to present a more meaningful discussion in this volume. I also offer my thanks to Marcus M. Mills for his line drawing illustrations and to Chuck Anderson and Jerome Thompson for permission to use their photographs.

2. Eugene N. Hastie, *High Points of Iowa History* (Perry, Iowa, 1966), pp. 37, 40–41, 43, 45, 46.

3. Hubert L. Moeller, *Hawkeye Tales* (Lake Mills, Iowa, 1963), pp. 17–20.

4. Don Doyle Brown, *Iowa, the Land across the River* (Des Moines, Iowa: Wallace-Homestead Co., 1963), pp. xv–xvi.

5. Jessie M. Dwelle. *Iowa Beautiful Land: A History of Iowa* (Mason City, Iowa: Klipto Loose Leaf Co., 1958), p. 13.

6. Charles Reuben Keyes, "Prehistoric Man in Iowa," *The Palimpsest* 8 (1927): 185–229.

7. Charles Reuben Keyes, "Prehistoric Indians in Iowa," *The Palimpsest* 32 (1951): 285–344.

8. Hubert L. Moeller and Hugh C. Moeller, *Our Iowa: Its Beginnings and Growth* (New York: Newson and Co., 1938), p. 23.

9. Brown, *Land across the River*, p. xvii.

10. Keyes, "Prehistoric Man in Iowa," pp. 185–86.

11. Robert Silverberg, *Mound Builders of Ancient America: The Archaeology of a Myth* (Greenwich: New York Graphic Society, Ltd., 1968); R. Clark Mallam, "The Mound Builders: An American Myth," *Journal of the Iowa Archeological Society* 23 (1976): 145–75.

12. See Keyes, "Prehistoric Man in Iowa" and "Prehistoric Indians of Iowa"; Mildred Mott, "The Relation of Historic Indian Tribes and Archaeological Manifestations in Iowa," *Iowa Journal of History and Politics* 36 (1938): 277–314; Marshall B. McKusick, *Men of Ancient Iowa* (Ames: Iowa State University Press, 1964); Adrian D.

Anderson, "Review of Iowa River Valley Archaeology," *Prehistoric Investigations*, edited by Marshall McKusick (Iowa City: University of Iowa Department of Publication, 1971), pp. 24–52; David M. Gradwohl, "Archaeology of the Central Des Moines River Valley: A Preliminary Summary," *Aspects of Upper Great Lakes Anthropology: Papers in Honor of Lloyd A. Wilford*, edited by Elden Johnson (St. Paul: Minnesota Historical Society, 1974), pp. 90–102; Duane C. Anderson, *Western Iowa Prehistory* (Ames: Iowa State University Press, 1975).

13. The matter of appropriate labels for Native American groups through time is extremely complex and admittedly risky. A good illustration of these problems is seen through Mildred Mott Wedel's recent discussion of the "Dakota" on the basis of the journals of Pierre-Charles LeSueur, "LeSueur and the Dakota Sioux," *Aspects of Upper Great Lakes Anthropology*, pp. 157–71. Ultimately, problems arise from at least three bases: (1) the actual fission and fusion of sociopolitical groups in the eighteenth and nineteenth centuries, (2) inaccuracies and misunderstandings on the part of Euro-American observers, and (3) differing preferences on the part of Native Americans during the nineteenth and twentieth centuries. The situation continues today as illustrated by the differing in-group labels employed by Native American students and participants in recent symposia at Iowa State University.

14. Adrian Anderson and Joseph A. Tiffany, "Rummells-Maske: A Clovis Findspot in Iowa," *Plains Anthropologist* 17 (1972): 55–59.

15. Richard Shutler, Duane C. Anderson et al., "The Cherokee Sewer Site (13CK405): A Preliminary Report of a Stratified Paleo-Indian/Archaic Site in Northwestern Iowa," *Journal of the Iowa Archaeological Society* 21 (1974): 1–175.

16. W. D. Frankforter, "A Pre-ceramic Site in Western Iowa," *Journal of the Iowa Archaeological Society* 8 (1959): 47–68; George Agogino and W. D. Frankforter, "A Paleo Bison-kill in Northwestern Iowa," *American Antiquity* 25 (1960): 414–15.

17. See Adrian D. Anderson, "Review of Iowa River Archaeology"; Elaine Bluhm Herold, "Hopewell: Burial Mound Builders," *The Palimpsest* 51 (1970): 497–528; Wilfred D. Logan, "Analysis of Woodland Complexes in Northeastern Iowa," dissertation, University of Michigan, 1958; Stuart Streuver, "The Hopewell Interaction Sphere in Riverine-Western Great Lakes Culture History," *Hopewellian Studies* (Springfield: Illinois State Museum Scientific Papers 12, 1964), pp. 85–106; and "Middle Woodland Culture History in the Great Lakes Riverine Area," *American Antiquity* 31 (1965): 211–23.

18. Today the Mesquakie still build structures of this architectural form which they call *wickiups*. The Algonquian terms *wickiup* and *wigwam* are both used in the literature pertaining to this house form in the eastern woodlands, although the former term is often applied to the grass- or brush-covered shelters built in the western basin-plateau areas by such groups as the Shoshone and Apache.

19. Adrian D. Anderson, "The Glenwood Sequence," *Journal of the Iowa Archaeological Society* 10 (1961): 1–101; David M. Gradwohl, *Prehistoric Villages in Eastern Nebraska* (Lincoln, Nebraska: Nebraska State Historical Society, 1969).

20. John C. Ives, "Mill Creek Pottery," *Journal of the Iowa Archaeological Society* 11 (1962): 1–126; Dale R. Henning, "Climatic Change and the Mill Creek Culture of Iowa," *Journal of the Iowa Archaeological Society* 15 (1968): 1–191 and 16 (1969): 192–358; Duane C. Anderson, "Mill Creek Culture: A Review," *Plains Anthropologist* 14 (1969): 137–43.

21. See Elden Johnson, "Decorative Motifs on Great Oasis Pottery," *Plains Anthropologist* 14 (1969): 272–76; Dale R. Henning, "Great Oasis Culture Distributions," *Prehistoric Investigations*, pp. 125–33; and David M. Gradwohl, "Archaeology of the Central Des Moines River Valley."

22. Mildred Mott Wedel, "Oneota Sites on the Upper Iowa River," *Missouri Archaeologist* 21 (1959): 1–181; Dale R. Henning, "Development and Interrelationships of Oneota Culture in the Lower Missouri River Valley," *Missouri Archaeologist* 32 (1970): 1–180; Marshall B. McKusick, *The Grant Oneota Village* (Iowa City: University of Iowa Department of Publications, 1973); and David M. Gradwohl, "Archaeology of the Central Des Moines River Valley."

23. The best documentation of certain specific linkages in Iowa has been presented by Mildred Mott Wedel, who argues for a less generalized association than that presented here (see Mildred Mott, "The Relation of Historic Indian Tribes and Archaeological Manifestations in Iowa" and Mildred Mott Wedel, "Oneota Sites on the Upper Iowa River"). The entire demonstration of these linkages is extremely complex and clearly outside the bounds of this chapter, aimed at an essentially lay audience. Here I am, frankly, glossing over some issues relating to taxonomic classifications and ethnographic identifications important to, and not agreed upon by, professional archaeologists. Specialists should consult further some of the more primary sources cited in this chapter and should note that the Ioway have been linked with the Orr Focus, the proto-Ioway-Oto are suggested to be represented by Correctionville-Blue Earth components, while the Missouri are thought to be associated with still other archaeological manifestations within the Oneota Tradition as it is generally construed. Outside Iowa, complexes designated as Oneota (or Plains Oneota) have been linked to groups other than Chiwere, in particular certain Dhegiha-Siouan speakers.

24. Herbert J. Muller, *The Uses of the Past* (New York: Mentor Books, 1952), p. 389.

5 Mesquakie History
As We Know It

BERTHA WASESKUK

As previously discussed, the foresight of the Mesquakie and the sensitive fairness of the legislature of the state of Iowa in 1856 are virtually unique in the pages of American governmental and Indian history. The episodes of the last century, movingly described here by Bertha Waseskuk, provide a basis for fathoming some of the matters discussed in Chapter 7 by Donald Wanatee.

Waseskuk is a member of the Mesquakie tribe. She states, "This account was compiled and translated from the writings of early Mesquakie historians. It is intended only to bring out interesting Mesquakie history as we know it. The account is not complete, the condition of some of the notebooks making it impossible to read the older style of handwriting."

Waseskuk approaches the subject of Mesquakie history from a personal and philosophical (really existential) perspective. The account here is more a folk history than a critical archivally based perspective such as Purcell's Chapter 3. Waseskuk's narrative is a combination of selected written documents and oral traditions handed down from generation to generation among the Mesquakie.

We always had plenty; our children never cried from hunger, neither were our people in want. . . . The rapids of Rock River furnished us with an abundance of excellent fish, and the land being very fertile, never failed to produce good crops. . . . Here our village stood for more than a hundred years, during all of which time we were the undisputed possessors of the Mississippi Valley. . . . Our village was healthy and there was no place in the country possessing such advantages. . . . If a prophet had come to our village in those days and told us that the things were to take place which have since come to pass, none of our people would have believed him.
— Black Hawk (Ma-Ka-Tai-Me-She-Kia-Kiak), Sauk

I am a Mesquakie — my Creator made me in his own likeness and he made this country for me. My Creator placed me on this earth and laid down laws by which I should live. He gave me my religion by which I might worship him so that I might dwell forever in the Hereafter that he has prepared for me. My Creator loves me and reminds

This chapter is a slightly edited and abridged version of a longer account included in the 1966 program of the 51st Mesquakie Indian Pow Wow, originally distributed in dittoed form.

me of his love at all times by being around me. I see him in Grand-mother Earth who gives me my food, both wild and from the seed I plant. I see him in the sun from whom I receive warmth and health. I see him in the trees around me from whence I get material for shelter, bark and roots for my medicine, and wood for my fire. In the rivers and streams he has placed fish and turtle for me. Wild game and fowl are always plentiful so that I might have plenty to eat.

Because my Creator called this my country, and because his love for me is always apparent, I have been a subject of intense hatred and jeal-ousy among other tribes and nations. I have suffered almost certain extermination at the hands of other Indian tribes several times.

My written history is fragmentary at best. My early historians wrote down events only now and then, and they did not always write down the most important things. The Mesquakie's early association with the White settlers is borne out by the fact that my early writers adopted sixteen letters of the English alphabet. The letters, put together in different combinations, form phrases and clauses in the Mesquakie language.

One of the earliest entries of the first writers tells of the battle in which other Indian tribes attempted to annihilate me. The affair was so horrifying and at the same time so infuriating that as soon as I got back on my feet I went back and wiped out two tribes. I was once a great and mighty nation. As the shield of Christian Great Britain dis-plays the lion, Russia has its bear. And as the seal of the United States of Christian civilization has the eagle, so upon the shields of my nation was found my totem, the head of a fox.

About 1700 I controlled the region south and west of Lake Michi-gan. The French traders of Canada descending the Mississippi River and those of Louisiana ascending the river to pass up the Illinois and Kankakee rivers had to pay me toll to cross my territory. This angered the French so they decided to destroy me, for they thought that in no other way could the communication between Louisiana and Canada be kept open. To this end, in 1712 various western tribes were asked by the commandant in Detroit to come and settle near the fort. I, the Mesquakie, was invited to come and camp with them. Gradually other tribes moved around until they had surrounded me. I told them that whatever they were plotting to remember that my Creator knew me and loved me and that they would not have their own way. Here the first step of attempted annihilation was taken. A siege of many days followed, and council was denied me. One foggy night I escaped but my enemies overtook me and I had to surrender to merciless odds.

Two times after this, the French tried without success to carry out their nefarious plot. In 1730 they made an all-out effort to destroy the Creator's beloved Mesquakie. For half a century at almost regular intervals, the jealous and hate-inflamed fellow inhabitants of my beautiful country were denied their wish — they who were created after me and some of them by deities lesser than my Creator! Still they did not realize that only a power higher than man could have kept them from accomplishing this deed. For I knew then, as I know now, that I shall live and cease to live with this country my Creator has made for me. In a manner known only to me, he interfered so that the combined forces of the French and several Indian tribes could not have their way with my tribe. The Mesquakie managed to pull together after repeated attacks.

My braves had put away their bow and arrow to forget the century just passed — a century of struggle for survival — but it seemed that there were other plans to be fulfilled. My village was then at the present location of Dubuque, Iowa. It was revealed to me, in a vision, that I should have a friend. He would come from the direction of the sunrise. I should go to him, and I would know him by this manner: he would have a light skin and blue eyes and he would have hair around his mouth. He would know me for he also had been told that he would have a friend, and that he would know him for the friend who would come to find him.

So it was that a party of my braves left for the east to contact him who was to be my friend, for I had no friends among my fellow inhabitants. When I reached his camp, he was at war. Leaving my companions a short distance away, I entered his camp alone. Although he had been expecting me, he was surprised to see me. He did not know that I was there until I tapped him on the shoulder. He asked me how I had got to him, as the country was covered with heavy artillery and soldiers were everywhere. He remarked that I could not have flown nor traveled below ground. I answered him that I had walked around his artillery and stepped over his sleeping soldiers. We did not have trouble meeting as friends.

My early writers emphasize that the Mesquakie did not engage in war with the settlers. Some entries even say that the Mesquakie helped fight off the other tribes when they attacked small White parties as they moved west toward open country.

It seems that Mesquakie was more interested in nurturing the friendship of the White settler. Many people familiar with the Mesquakie history have wondered why the Mesquakie, while a vicious enemy to the Indian tribes, was always friendly to the Whites. Notes taken on the Lewis and Clark expedition read in part concerning the Mesquakies (referred to as the Renards by the French and translated in English as the Fox):

They raise an abundance of corn, beans, and squash; they sometimes hunt in the country west of them toward the Missouri but their principal hunting [was] on both sides of the Mississippi, from the mouth of the Wisconsin River to the mouth of the Illinois River. These people are extremely friendly to the Whites and seldom injure their traders; but they are the most implacable enemies to the Indian nations with whom they are at war; to them is justly attributable the almost entire destruction of the Missouries, Illinois, Cahokias, Kaskaskias, and Peorias.

The Treaty of 1804 (Article 4) reads: "The United States will never interrupt the said tribes in the possession of lands which they rightfully claim, but will, on the contrary, protect them in the quiet enjoyment of the same, against their own citizens and against all other White persons, who may intrude upon them"— signed, William Henry Harrison. At the outbreak of the War of 1812, the president of the United States contacted the Mesquakie, advised him to remain neutral, to stay home, and to raise food for his children.

In 1815 the Treaty of Ghent was entered into by Great Britain and the United States. Under Article 9 the parties agreed to call off the war with the Indians. The Indian tribes along the Mississippi were mainly involved. In this connection the United States entered into treaties with the different tribes. The Mesquakie, being located along the Mississippi, also entered into a treaty. But besides the four articles formally included in the document, a spokesman, Ma-Ka-Te-We-Ne-Ne-Me-Ki-Wa (Black Thunder), on behalf of the Mesquakie chief entered into a special agreement with the commissioners of the United States, William Clark, Ninian Edwards, and August Choteau. These agreements were oral, and while they have never been honored by the

United States, they have been handed down for eventual use. Article 2 of the separate treaty with the Mesquakie dealt with "perpetual friendship and peace between the United States of America and all individuals of the Fox tribe or nation."

So matters stood when a Sac warrior decided to defy the pressure brought on by the Treaty of 1804 at St. Louis. The treaty was a farce! On the Indian side of the ledger, it was unjust, illegal, and unofficial. The Sac warrior knew this, and in knowing it, found it hard to abide. His grazing land was increasingly plowed up and planted with corn by the Whites. When he turned out his ponies, they trampled on the White man's crops. No matter which way he turned, he was hemmed in. He was suffocated by the fast closing in of the White tide — a feeling known only to a people who have enjoyed true freedom.

Na-E-Di-A was chief of the Mesquakie Nation and he had his principal village on the present site of Davenport, Iowa, just across the river from where Black Hawk made his unsuccessful stand. After the Sac warrior was defeated, and another treaty was forced on him, the United States government invited the Mesquakie chiefs to come to Washington, D.C., to go over existing treaties and arrange for settlement under their terms. Mesquakie historians show that sixteen chiefs, warriors, and principal speakers undertook the journey. Somewhere along the way, the group was attacked by a large band of Menominee Indians. The ambush seemed, at the time, to be without reason. Later, however, it was apparent that the ambush had been planned.

Some of the important Mesquakie treaties were lost in the affray. It was thought then that the United States government was a party to the plan. After the ambush seven of the original group returned. All the chiefs, however, had been killed. A temporary chief had to be chosen, for the sons of those that were killed were all minors and were not ready to take up leadership of their people. As the pipe was passed around the council to determine who should act as chief, a woman (Ma-Que-Ka) accepted it and named her brother Pow-E-Shiek to be temporary chief. Thus he became chief in name only, rather than by heredity as is the custom among the Mesquakie. Bad judgment often causes hardship for a people. At a time when the reins of this tribe should have been kept taut, they were thrown into the hands of one who put personal glory ahead of duty. The temporary leader, along with the Sac chief, Keokuk, signed away a great territory without permission from all their tribesmen. They then made their way to Kansas with those who would follow them.

They remained in Kansas for two years. Many followers were dying from an epidemic. The others were homesick for the woodlands along the Iowa River and the rich black soil. The government was urging them with considerable pressure to divide the reservation land into individual plots. There was discontent among the people. Their leaders had brought dissatisfaction and illness to the group; they had signed away millions of acres of land. So the temporary leader gave the chief-ship back to whom it belonged, to the hereditary successor, Ma-Me-Nwa-Ne-Ke, who was now ready to take up his duties as leader of the Mesquakie tribe.

In the early 1850s, the United States government sent to Kansas a special agent to bring about Ma-Me-Nwa-Ne-Ke's return to Iowa. The young chief had been in control of his people in Kansas for seven years when the special agent arrived there. Several Indian tribes were encamped near the Mesquakie pending further agreements with the government for their removal to the south and west into what is now Oklahoma. The agent, having found the Mesquakie section of the encampment, asked six different tribal groups before he was satisfied that he had found his party.

Records reveal his search to have been a secret affair, and he discretely contacted the young chief. Under cover of night the agent instructed him in what he was to say at a general council the next day. So it was that Ma-Me-Nwa-Ne-Ke elected to turn back to Iowa instead of agreeing to go on south with the other tribes. Ma-Me-Nwa-Ne-Ke then had his followers take up a collection of money. When this was done, he sent his brother Pa-Ta-Co-To and several of his council to journey to Iowa to effect a purchase of land that would be the home of the Mesquakie and his heirs forever. As the Creator provided a beautiful fertile country for the people of his image, so the Mesquakie chiefs acquired a portion of the beautiful Iowa land for their children and their children's children for all time to come.

The Iowa Assembly subsequently passed an act permitting certain Indians to reside within the state:

> Be it enacted by the General Assembly of the State of Iowa, that the consent of the State is hereby given that the Indians now residing

in Tama County known as a portion of the Sac and Foxes, be permitted to remain and reside in said State, and that the Governor be requested to inform the Secretary of War thereof, and urge on said department the propriety of paying said Indians their proportion of the annuities due or to become due to said tribes.

Sec. 2. That the sheriff of said county, shall as soon as a copy of this law is filed in the office of the County Court proceed to take the census of said Indians now residing there giving their names and sex, which said list shall be filed and recorded in said office, the persons whose names are included in said list shall have the privileges granted under this act, but none others shall be considered as embraced within the provisions of said act.

Sec. 3. This act shall take effect from and after its publication in the Iowa City Reporter and Iowa City Republican published at Iowa City.

Approved July 15, 1856.
I certify that the foregoing act was published in the Iowa Capital Reporter July 20th and in the Iowa City Republican July 23rd, 1856. Signed Geo. W. McCleary, Secretary of State.

Seven hundred and thirty-five dollars were collected and brought to Iowa from Kansas for the purchase of land. The price of the first tract bought was one thousand dollars. The amount was made up by granting the parties who were selling the tract their request to be permitted to cut down standing timber. On a later purchase the landowners wanted some of the Mesquakie's ponies. The chief allowed them to pick the ponies they wanted, then he replaced the ones taken from his braves with his own ponies. Only ponies belonging to members of the Mesquakie people were used and only Mesquakie people were allowed to contribute to the money collected.

After the initial purchase was effected, the chief's brother Pa-Ta-Co-To sent a party back to Kansas to inform Chief Ma-Me-Nwa-Ne-Ke that all was ready. The state of Iowa issued the following statement:

The bearers, Don-nah, Au-shu-tan, Tep-pes-su-pen-a-hut, and Kee-she-que are the representatives of a portion of a tribe of Indians known as Mesquakies or Sac and Foxes living in Tama County, Iowa, by permission of State authority as provided in the above act of the legislature. These Indians are peaceable and friendly to the Government of the United States. They are now on a visit to a portion of their tribe now in Kansas and desire to pass unmolested.

They represent that Nan-mee-nee-wau-na-ke, Nan-a-wau-pit, and Nan-nah-ke-ah are heads of families or chiefs now in Kansas that formerly lived in Tama County, Iowa, and are entitled to the benefit of the foregoing act of the General Assembly of State of Iowa and that they with their families, and none others, may be permitted to quietly and peaceably return to their home and friends in Tama County. They fear that there may be hostile demonstrations upon the part of some of the western tribes of Indians and that their friends, owing to their close proximity to other western tribes, may be implicated. They therefore appeal to the Union friends of the country to aid them in placing their friends in a position that their true character may be understood.

The heads of chiefs of this tribe appeal to their white friends not to permit whiskey or intoxicating drinks to be sold or given to their returning friends as they feel responsible for their good behavior and therefore insist they be not allowed the use of anything that can intoxicate.

State of Iowa ss, I hereby certify that I am well acquainted with the first four Indians named in the foregoing instrument of writing and am well satisfied that they are a portion of the Indians entitled to the benefits of the law hereunto attached, that they and their tribe are on terms of the best friendship with our government.

Great Seal of
the State of Iowa

In testimony whereof I have hereunto set my hand and affixed the great seal of the State of Iowa.

Done at Des Moines this 10th day of Sept. 1861.
Elijah Sells, Sec'y of State
by Jno. M. Davis, Dep.

The Mesquakie did not straggle back in small numbers as some have stated. The first and main move was made by eleven households and numbered seventy-six Indians. At the same time here in Iowa, from one of the several camps, a tribal runner was sent to the camps of those who had not followed Pow-E-Shiek into Kansas. These later camps were located along the Cedar River and at the site of the present Amana Colonies. The runner was instructed to inform these Indians that their chief had bought land and that they were to move and join the main group at the new home. Thus ended the unsettled life of the Mesquakie, a turbulent history now forgotten, a terrific struggle for survival of the Creator's people.

6 The Red Earth People in 1905

A Photographic Essay

photographs from the collection of

D U R E N J. H. W A R D

The photographs, reproduced here with the permission of the Iowa State Historical Department/Division of the State Historical Society, are part of a collection assembled by Duren J. H. Ward, who spent two months at the Mesquakie Indian Settlement during the summer of 1905. Ward — a Canadian who was educated at Hillsdale College, Harvard University, and Leipzig University — was a Unitarian minister, lecturer, and anthropologist in Iowa City at the turn of the century. Under the auspices of the State Historical Society, Ward undertook a systematic recording of the history and culture of the Mesquakie. Ward's notes and photographs of the Mesquakie were turned over to the Historical Society, where they remained virtually unknown in files until 1973. At that time they were "rediscovered" and prepared for a traveling exhibit first shown at the Mesquakie Settlement during January 1974. These photographs supplement the images of the Mesquakies presented elsewhere in this book by Bertha Waseskuk and Donald Wanatee.

somewhere inside me,
there is a memory
of my grandfathers
catching robins
in the night
of early spring.
the snow continues
to gather children
outside, and i think,
as long as they are moving.
the frost sets itself
on the window before
the old man's eye.
we sit together
and imagine designs
which will eventually
vanish when the room
and talk become warm.
he goes over the people,
one by one. . . .
— from "Coming Back Home" by Ray Young Bear, Mesquakie

Born in 1833, Kwi ya ma is reported to have been one of the Mesquakies involved in warfare with the Comanche and other Plains tribes during the Mesquakies' decade of residence in Kansas. Photo courtesy State Historical Society of Iowa — Iowa City.

Push e to ne qua, born in 1842 near Homestead, Iowa, became the dominant Mesquakie leader in 1882. He was designated tribal chief by the federal government in the 1890s and was at the center of controversy over the issue of the Toledo, Iowa, Indian school. Photo courtesy State Historical Society of Iowa — Iowa City.

Ko ta to, born in 1890, was the second oldest child in a family of six. Photo courtesy State Historical Society of Iowa — Iowa City.

Mu kwa pu shi to, the claimant to tribal leadership, is shown in the late 1890s or the first years of the 1900s in the usual male Mesquakie attire of string turban and trade shirt. Photo courtesy State Historical Society of Iowa — Iowa City.

This madonna-like photo of Wa wa ki ki and child has been heavily retouched in this version and was a favorite with publishers of early twentieth-century picture postcards. Photo courtesy State Historical Society of Iowa — Iowa City.

This formal family portrait of the James Poweshiek (Pa wa shi ka) family (circa 1900) was probably taken in the studio of a Toledo, Iowa, photographer. James Poweshiek claimed to be the grandson of famed Mesquakie tribal leader Poweshiek and was for a time the United States policeman on the Settlement. Photo courtesy State Historical Society of Iowa — Iowa City.

Shown here is the Mesquakie tribal council (circa 1900). Seated in the center is Push e to ne qua, who had assumed a leadership role in the early 1880s. He was recognized by the United States government as chief in the 1890s. To his left is Ha na wa ta and to his right is Wa pa nu ke. Standing in the rear, left to right, are Na sa pi pya ta, Me skwa pu swa, and Wai to ne siwa. Photo courtesy State Historical Society of Iowa — Iowa City.

The Settlement (circa 1900). Photo courtesy State Historical Society of Iowa — Iowa City.

A scene on the Settlement along the Iowa River (circa 1905). Photo courtesy State Historical Society of Iowa — Iowa City.

The Wa she ta na kwa twa (George Morgan) family. Photo courtesy State Historical Society of Iowa — Iowa City.

7 The Lion, Fleur-de-lis, the Eagle, or the Fox

A Study of Government

DONALD WANATEE

In this chapter Donald Wanatee picks up strands of Indian history and culture that are part of the fabric of previous statements by Purcell and Waseskuk. Wanatee weaves the Mesquakie story into the contemporary scene — a matter, according to Purcell, left mute in most textbooks on Iowa history. Here Wanatee describes the hereditary basis of traditional Mesquakie government, a linkage of kinship and political systems quite different from the "American" system of government. He explains the historical evolution of certain social and political factions among the Mesquakie and offers some insights into the present ramifications of these problems. While Wanatee's case study is specifically on the Mesquakie, the matters he keenly observes are paralleled consistently throughout the contemporary Native American realm.

We did not think of the great open plains, the beautiful rolling hills, and winding streams with tangled growth, as "wild." Only to the white man was nature a "wilderness" and only to him was the land "infested" with "wild" animals and "savage" people. To us it was tame. Earth was bountiful and we were surrounded with the blessings of the Great Mystery. Not until the hairy man from the east came and with brutal frenzy heaped injustices upon us and the families we loved was it "wild" for us. When the very animals of the forest began fleeing from his approach, then it was that for us the "wild west" began.
—Luther Standing Bear, Oglala Sioux

THE RELATIONSHIP OF SOCIAL STRUCTURE AND POLITICAL ORGANIZATION AMONG INDIAN GROUPS

There are many planes of culture among the Indians and each one is characterized by widely varying forms of governance, from the simplest family group and small village community to the most complex confederation of some highly organized tribes. However, generally speaking, the basis of all the governments is the kinship system —

Acknowledgment is made to John Collier (*The Indians of the Americas*, New York: New American Library, 1947) for historical and background data used in this chapter.

consisting of groups of the same blood relationship, tracing descent through the male or female line.

The various sociopolitical units are the family, the clan (or gens), the phratry, the tribe, and the confederation — the latter two being the units most completely organized for governance. A confederation of tribes was quite unusual historically because the numerous conflicting interests of the individual tribes could not be adjusted without sacrifices that appeared to overbalance the benefits of a permanent confederation. Therefore among most American Indians tribal government prevailed as the basic sociopolitical organization.

Within tribal government organization, military functions were kept quite apart from civil functions. The civil government consisted of a chosen body of men called clan leaders or "chiefs," and of these there were several grades. These chiefs organized so that certain ones could concern themselves with legislative functions, others with judicial functions, and still others with executive functions, all pertaining to tribal welfare. Civil chiefs were not selected by virtue of their accomplishments in military activities, and if one of the civil chiefs chose to go to war he would usually resign from his civil functions.

In most tribal societies each and every structural unit had the right to hold a council. The chiefs of the clans were the tribal chiefs and they formed the tribal council. They voted, not individually, not by clans, but by phratries: groups of associated clans. This complicated system was necessary for conducting parliamentary business since Indian people generally ignore the principle of rule by majority, instead requiring absolute unanimity. The chiefs of a clan having agreed upon a course of action would then consult the wishes of the representatives of their sister clans. After concurring among themselves they could usually come to an agreement with the other opposing phratry. One dissenting voice of a single chief, however, could obstruct the work of the council. During times of great emergencies a grand council could also be held and this might consist of chiefs, subchiefs, matrons, head warriors, and other leading men of the tribe. One can see how family councils, clan or gens councils, tribal councils, and further, even confederation councils, would respectively exercise voice in separate and independent jurisdictions. Where confederacies were involved, it was necessary to take the further step of organizing a confederate council, and this formed the ruling body of the league.

With the entrance of the White man on the North American continent, the policies of the several governments toward the Indian peoples and their methods of pursuing them were often at variance. Governments other than those of the United States and the colonies that had control of various parts of this territory were Great Britain, France, Spain, Russia, Denmark, Sweden, and the Netherlands. The policies adopted by them in relation to Indian peoples differed in some ways, but all agreed in assuming the right of dominion, based on discovery, with no regard to the native Americans residing therein. In all the competition between the European nations regarding their claims to territory, the rights of Indians were not allowed to intervene. Although each government insisted on the right of dominion in its acquired territory, the rights of the original inhabitants were in but a few cases entirely disregarded or necessarily curtailed to a degree (*Johnson and Grahams' lessee* v. *McIntosh*, 8 Wheaton, 583 et. seg.). The Indians were admitted to be the rightful occupants of the lands, with rights of possession over that which was necessary for their use. The policies of the various governments, however, differed in the extent to which the exercise of this right was conceded. Spain limited it to lands actually occupied or used, while the United States usually allowed it to the land claimed.

The United States and other governments dealt with the Indians as "tribes." In the Articles of Confederation, "sole and exclusive right and power of regulating the trade and managing all affairs with Indians" was given to Congress, with the exception of those being under state jurisdiction. In the Constitution, Congress was granted the power to "regulate commerce with foreign nations and among the several states and with the Indian tribes." The term "tribes," as quoted, would indicate that the framers of the Constitution wished to deal with the Indian peoples as autonomous groups. This method was followed by the government until the act of March 3, 1871, which brought under immediate control of Congress (as specified in Article 1, Section 8, Clause 3, of the Constitution) all transactions with the Indians and thus reduced to simple agreements what had before been solemn treaties.

When Congress created the War Department in 1789, among the duties assigned therein were those "relative to Indian Affairs." These involved mostly financial matters of appropriations for annuities, warrants and requisitions on the same, and the handling of all correspondence with superintendents, agents, and subagents. In 1832 a Commissioner of Indian Affairs was created in the War Department, but not until 1834 was an act passed "to provide for the organization of the Department of Indian Affairs." When the Department of the Interior was created by the act of March 3, 1849, the Bureau of Indian Affairs was transferred therein and hence passed from military control into civil control.

Surpassing all other difficulties in ways of carrying out a just, humane, and consistent policy toward Indian peoples has been the antagonism born of the ignorance of both races of each other's mode of thought, customs, social ideals, and structure. Their assumptions in respect to land were and still are prominent factors. In a minority report of the House Committee (1880) one conviction expressed was as follows: "From the time of the discovery of America, and for centuries probably before that, the North American Indian has been a communist. Not in the offensive sense of modern communism, but in the sense of holding property in common. The very idea of property in the soil was unknown to the Indian mind. This communistic idea has grown into their very being and is an integral part of the Indian character. From our point of view this is all wrong; but it is folly to think of uprooting it through agency or a mere act of Congress or by the establishment of a theoretical policy."[1] John Collier, in his report, explained a way of governing the Indian tribes under a "soviet plan" that permits the tribes to retain their own way of governing and yet be integrated into the United States government. In this plan, based actually upon a true communism type of government, the various Indian tribes practicing this unanimity would be afforded the chance to regain their own self-governing policies and to become self-functioning bodies.

SHIFTING MESQUAKIE SYSTEMS DURING THE
EIGHTEENTH AND NINETEENTH CENTURIES

Based on the previous discussion of different sociopolitical structures and differing legal prerogatives, I want to delve into the existence of the Mesquakie tribe residing here in Iowa and its relationship with the invading Euro-Americans. It was the Europeans who first called the Mesquakies "Renards" or "the Fox."

The Mesquakies entered White man's history in 1636. When the first French traders came upon them, they numbered two thousand and were living near Green Bay, Wisconsin. The Mesquakies, not given to subservience to the Euro-American encroachments, were involved in a series of disastrous wars with the French and France's Indian allies. At one time they were reduced to only a few families. They regained a foothold, however, and by the eighteenth century Mesquakie numbers had returned to the original two thousand. In 1734 the Mesquakies made a political alliance with the Sacs. This alliance remained in force for some one hundred years although the two tribes continued to maintain separate camps. After the American Revolution, the pressure of settlers steadily increased and the Mesquakies and Sacs moved south and west along the Mississippi River. At the beginning of the Black Hawk War in 1831, the Mesquakies moved across the Mississippi River into Iowa. Fifteen years later the United States army removed the Mesquakies as well as the Sacs from Iowa and placed them on a government reservation in Kansas.

In Kansas, in 1856, the Mesquakie and Sac tribes came to an open split over issues of acculturation. Attempts were made by the government agent to encourage White agricultural techniques by allotting the reservation lands to individuals. The Mesquakies, led by their hereditary chief Maminiwanige, who had not been recognized by the United States government, consistently opposed the division of the communal lands. When their opposition proved to be of no avail, some Mesquakies removed from the reservation.

Under the leadership of Maminiwanige, a band of five Mesquakie men were sent back to their former homelands in Iowa to search for a place to live. A sum of money was raised from the sale of ponies, and 80 acres of timberland were purchased on the Iowa River. Permission to settle there was obtained from the governor of Iowa. Mesquakies who had earlier separated from the tribe and had never left Iowa now rejoined this group, and Mesquakies in Kansas also returned a few at a time. In 1856 a resolution was passed by the Iowa legislature permitting the Mesquakies to reside herein, so long as they remained at peace.

The federal government, however, treated the Mesquakies as renegades and paid no annuities to them until eleven years later. Then, by an act of Congress, they were granted a pro rata share of the annuities of the united Sac and Mesquakie tribe and an agent was appointed to pay these annuities. However, legal jurisdiction and trusteeship over these lands were still held by the state of Iowa which, aside from the collection of taxes on the lands, stayed well apart from tribal affairs. During this absence of federal administration the Mesquakies were effectively self-governing and relationships with Whites were largely on an individual basis.

In 1881 Maminiwanige died and was replaced by Pushetonequa. Moquibushito, the son and hereditary heir of the former chief, was set aside by the council as being too young and incompetent to inherit the chieftainship. This decision was generally accepted by the tribe at that time as a legitimate council action.

PROBLEMS INHERITED BY THE TWENTIETH CENTURY

In 1896 jurisdiction over the Mesquakies was resumed by the federal government, except that the state of Iowa retained its right to establish highways and levy taxes. From that time on continuous efforts have been made to force White ways of thinking and acting upon Mesquakies. This transfer of authority to the federal government brought about a significant change in the position of the Mesquakies. Previous to this they were free to accept or reject elements of White culture, but now they found themselves in a position of definite subordination to the power of the federal agent. Hence, the Mesquakies were shifted from a position of substantial political equality with their White neighbors to one in which they were under a separate law, administered by a member of the White community.

In 1898 Pushetonequa and three members of the council were asked to come to Washington to speak with the Commissioner of Indian Affairs about the situation at the boarding school. The school was built a year earlier in Toledo, Iowa, and only four children were enrolled. Pushetonequa was offered an annual salary of five hundred dollars and federal recognition of his chieftainship in exchange for his cooperation in enrolling the children. A month later Pushetonequa accepted the offer, and he and several councilmen enrolled their children in the school.

When the "government chief," Pushetonequa, accepted White support and used his influence to support the school, an opposing faction (having been in existence since Pushetonequa's appointment) sprang forth in full support of Moquibushito, the hereditary heir to the chieftainship. This political situation resulted in the formation of two factions: one around the kin of Moquibushito and one around Pushetonequa, with federal authority recognizing the latter as "chief."

The factional split, having been precipitated by the acculturation issue, became more pronounced as time passed. Pushetonequa was now chief by the grace of federal power and received his annual salary from the federal government. He and his kinsmen leaned more and more toward White political support and White values.

In 1910 the government agents sought to persuade the Mesquakie to allot their lands to individuals to encourage "individual initiative." A group of young highly acculturated Mesquakie men of the Pushetonequa faction petitioned the agent for allotments, and later Pushetonequa agreed to allotments for the young men. The Old Bear faction (literal translation of Moquibushito) solidly opposed the program and they mustered sufficient support to prevent it. Also, the government lacked the power to force individual allotments since the land was tribally owned and not a federal reserve.

Pushetonequa died in 1919 and the federal government refused to recognize any successor. Therefore the Mesquakie tribal council continued to handle tribal affairs under the leadership of Pushetonequa's son Youngbear. The council functioned as a self-perpetuating oligarchy, with federal support, and its members were replaced with others of pro-White orientation.

ADDITIONAL POLITICAL PROBLEMS, 1930S—1950S

In 1937 the members of the Youngbear faction (Pushetonequa's descendents and followers), having become increasingly pro-White, managed to get the tribe's acceptance of the Wheeler-Howard Act. This act (also called the Indian Reorganization Act of 1934) provided for a representative government through an elected council of seven. The federal government endowed upon the tribe the name of "Sac and Fox (Mesquakies) Indians of the Mississippi of Iowa"— once more associating the Mesquakies with the Sacs in the alliance that had existed some one hundred years before and which had long since been disregarded as being in effect by the Mesquakies. The *elected* council also did not provide any recognition for positions relating to hereditary chieftainship, the very positions that formed the basis for the political and social integration and function of the Indian tribe. Youngbear—who now considered himself "heir" to the chieftainship—and members of the Youngbear faction accepted the situation and successfully ran for positions on the "elected" tribal council. The Old Bear faction continued to show no recognition to the "elected" tribal council. Therefore, Old Bear faction members did not vote in council elections.

As years passed, the Old Bear faction became so oppressed by an "Indian Court" established by the Youngbear faction holding office that a leader of the Old Bear faction initiated a petition calling for the abolition of the court. After collecting more than one hundred signatures, the Old Bear leader wrote to Iowa Congressman Gwynne complaining of the court and demanding that the hereditary chieftainship in the Old Bear line be reestablished. In 1943 the court was abolished.

In 1944 the Old Bear group elected to the council three of its members. Three years later the group again demanded in a letter to the Commissioner of Indian Affairs that recognition of the hereditary chieftainship be returned to them. Also in 1947 the Old Bear faction elected three new members to the council. In 1948 a delegation from the Old Bear faction, including most of the tribal council members, went to Washington to ask for revision of the tribal constitution in favor of hereditary chieftainship. While visiting in Washington the "secretary" of the delegation, a young kinswoman who had been educated at Tama High School and attended junior college for a short time, testified against a state jurisdiction bill then before Congress and she also visited the National Archives to examine treaties of the Sac and Fox with the United States. Upon the return of the delegation to the settlement, much publicity was given to the treaties under which large sums of money were, according to the "secretary," still due the Mesquakie tribe.

The Old Bear faction then hired a law firm to represent its case. In 1950 Jack Old Bear, the hereditary chief of the Mesquakies by the Old Bear lineage, filed suit in federal court at Cedar Rapids asking for a judgment giving him sole power to represent the tribe. He named as defendants the seven members of the tribal council at that time, most of whom were of the Youngbear faction. In addition, the seven members of the tribal council who were named as defendants had just started action in the name of the "Sac and Fox of the Mississippi of Iowa," presenting claims against the federal government for payment of lands they claimed the tribe had lost through force and fraud in years past, the claims covering nearly half a billion dollars. The Old Bear faction was opposed to the filing of these claims. However, the lawsuit brought by Jack Old Bear in Cedar Rapids was dismissed by Judge Henry Graven on the grounds that the suit was not within the jurisdiction of the federal district court. Judge Graven said that sections giving the federal court jurisdiction in Indian cases refer to other specified matters and that "this court has been referred to no statute, and it is unable to find any statute giving it jurisdiction in this case."[2]

So in 1950 the trend toward pro-White leadership, which had begun when Pushetonequa capitulated to the wants of the federal government fifty years previously, had been reversed. The Old Bear faction had now gained strong support. The factions still thought of themselves as pro-White and anti-White. The Youngbear faction had stopped resisting the White community and attempted to exchange Mesquakie values for acceptance by the Whites, but this acceptance was not given. The Mesquakies were suffering under economic and status deprivation. The Youngbear faction was blamed for these deprivations and lost followers. Yet the Mesquakies could not develop means for the legitimation of leaders capable of initiating action to do away with these deprivations. The elective system established by the Wheeler-Howard Act at the settlement in 1937 merely provided a more sensitive sounding board for factional conflict. The result has been the suffering of the Mesquakie people, being so divided against themselves that they cannot take coordinated action.

A FINAL PERSONAL PERSPECTIVE

I am a Mesquakie Indian, a member of the Old Bear faction, and have served as a member of the "Sac and Fox Tribal Council." I fully support the Old Bear faction in its desire to revise the tribal constitution and to install a council with a constitution that recognizes the hereditary chieftainship. I believe this would serve the needs of our people. We are a distinct cultural group with our own special needs in reference to a self-governing body.

Felix Cohen has pointed out some of the problems of self-government of Indians within the federal bureaucratic system. In his words, "The most basic of all Indian rights (the right to self-government) is the Indian's last defense against bureaucratic oppression, for in a realm where the states are powerless to govern and where Congress, occupied with more pressing national affairs, cannot govern wisely and well, there remains a large no-man's-land in which government can emanate only from officials of the Indian Department or from the Indians themselves."[3] However, what *form* of self-government is an area of debate. Are we to be forced to use the White man's form of government to be self-governing? Then this is not self-government. It will not work. It has not worked because our people cannot adapt to this form of government without sacrificing basic tenets of our social and political organization. The problem is one of relating Indian political forms to the general governmental framework of the United States without arbitrarily interfering with accepted customs and practices. I contend that, through legal council, we must fight for our right to be free to establish our own form of self-government and that this move is essential if we are to survive as a people.

It would be most interesting if we Mesquakies were allowed to form our own government. Is it possible for a communal-type government to exist and function well while remaining within the fold of the United States government, which is basically capitalistic in nature? We are determined to find out.

The Mesquakies and their society have disclosed that social heritage is far more perduring than is commonly believed. Perhaps no other ethnic group has revealed this old important truth so convincingly as the Mesquakie has done. This capacity for perdurance is one of the truths on which the hope of our world rests — our world grown so pale in the last century, and now so deathly pallid, through the totalitarian rule of some forms of government.

NOTES

1. Hearings before the Committee on Indian Affairs, House of Representatives, 73rd Congress, 2nd Session on H.R. 7902, part 9.

2. Tama newspaper, April 15, 1950.

3. "American Indians and American Life," *The Annals* 311 (May 1957): 119.

8 Urbanization of the American Indian
One Man's View

REUBEN SNAKE

Reuben Snake (Winnebago) is concerned about Indian children who grow up in urban areas such as Sioux City. His own experiences have made him aware of how easy it is for young people to lose sight of their heritage amid the concrete and steel of the city. In this chapter, as in the previous one, we are made aware of the complex problems Indians face when dealing with the social and governmental agencies of the White culture and the constant pressures Indians must exert to maintain even a semblance of self-determination.

Long ago they used to live wherever the elders stayed. They got along together harmoniously. None of them was at odds with another. In the beginning people loved each other.
— *Mountain Wolf Woman, Winnebago*

For Indian people living in the cities it is very difficult to maintain our veracity . . . our value system. This was one of the concerns we had in our program, the Indian Education Project, in Sioux City. For myself, I am going through a process of education too, since up to the time I was twenty-eight years old, most of my Indian culture came from listening to and watching the Lone Ranger and Tonto.

I knew I was Winnebago; I knew I was Siouan; I knew I was Red. But in all the years I went to school — BIA schools, public schools, mission schools — no one person ever told me what I should be proud of as an Indian. If anybody called me a dirty Indian or a damned Indian, I usually punched him in the mouth, because I was proud of being an Indian. But nobody ever told me what it was that I could be proud of.

The Sioux City Education Project puts a great deal of emphasis on this area of identity, because it is not going to mean a thing to us if we educate our children to become doctors, lawyers, engineers, philosophers, and orators if they lose their identity as Red people. That is why

This chapter excerpts remarks made by the author at the 1974 National Indian Education Association's Conference in Phoenix, Arizona, and the 1975 Symposium on the American Indian at Iowa State University.

we have recruited the strongest spiritual persons we could find to come and work with us.

In 1972 the regional office in Kansas City put together a task force of federal agency people and Indians from the four-state area of Missouri, Kansas, Iowa, and Nebraska that came to Sioux City and held a meeting with the various Indian organizations in the city asking them what their priorities were. The one organization in the Sioux City community that, at the time, listed education as a number one priority was the Sioux City chapter of the American Indian Movement. Members of this group asked me to come in as a technical consultant on the development of an education proposal. I was working in Albuquerque, New Mexico, at the time and I came up and we started formulating some ideas. Through a series of community meetings that included most of the Indian leaders and Indian representatives of Sioux City, we put together some ideas concerning an educational project. We submitted the proposal for funding during the year of the implementation of the Indian Education Act, but we did not get the project funded. This past year we resubmitted it and received one hundred thousand dollars of Title IV money to accomplish several things in the Sioux City community.

The first priority was the development of cultural education activities to help our Indian children who in some instances are second and third generation urban Indians. Being Indian in the twentieth century is a difficult job regardless of where you are, but it seems to be a little more difficult to be an Indian when you are living on a day-to-day basis amidst a lot of people who are not Indians. When you get Indian people whose families have been in the city for two or three generations, you find they have more or less lost contact with the culture and traditions of their people. So we have many young children running the streets of Sioux City who know nothing at all about their heritage, yet the system identifies them as Indians and expects them to be Indians and to act like Indians, but their concept of the way an Indian acts is a little bit different from more traditionally oriented people from the reservations. So we have some extreme problems in this area of helping young Indian children develop a positive identity for themselves. But this is one of the major efforts of our project. We have instituted a Sioux Indian language program in our center. There are seventeen tribal groups that have been identified as living in Sioux City. The Sioux is the largest, then the Winnebago and Omaha. And so we have a Siouan language class and a Northern Plains Indian singing group that we are getting started. We have brought into the community Indian center different people to assist us. We have had Sioux medicine men come and conduct Sioux ceremonies, pipe ceremonies, and other traditional activities to expose the Indian young people to some of the more meaningful aspects of being an Indian. But that is just one part of the job.

Another major effort of ours is to develop curriculum materials for the system. We hope these will not only support our Indian children in developing a positive identity but will also eradicate some of the negative feelings that are developed by most people through what we call education. We are trying to develop materials for history classes — American history and Iowa history — that are a little more factual and a little more honest and tell history as it really happened, dealing with the contributions that American Indians have made to the development of the country. We are also developing materials in social studies and we have some hopes of doing the same in music and physical education. It is a very difficult thing to do because not too many resources exist for the accumulation and the compilation of material to use in this way. More and more groups are getting into the business of curriculum development, but when you have to deal with tribal entities you cannot use something that was designed for the Chippewas, for the Iroquois, or the Southwest tribes. You cannot use the same materials for Winnebagos, Sioux, and Omahas. You have to work on developing material from those tribal backgrounds. We work with the Winnebago, the Omaha, the Santee, and Yankton Sioux tribes in putting this material together and we are to the point where we have a significant amount of material. Now we are trying to prepare ourselves to get this material into print. It is difficult to find people who have the talent to develop material for young children. We are looking for that kind of expertise to help us design the curriculum materials we need.

Another activity of our center is to provide supportive services to the Indian students to try to encourage them to hang in there. Many of our families in Sioux City, because they come from a poverty background, come from family situations where alcoholism might be a problem — or inadequate housing or unemployment. We have to provide them with the assistance to get a job, to get counseling, or to find adequate housing. It is an ongoing effort that continues to expand because many families continue to come to Sioux City. It seems as if every week there is a family that comes into Sioux City and comes to the center to ask for our help in finding a place to stay, in getting a job, or in getting some emergency assistance for food. So we are not dealing only with the people who have lived in the city for a number of years, but we are also dealing with a lot of people who are moving into the city. And so we spend a great deal of time in dealing with them. We have one staff member who spends the major part of his time working with the home-school liaison people and with other counseling staff in the schools trying to help children who may have a conflict with teachers or are not keeping up their attendance or perhaps are having some other kinds of problems within the school. And that is another activity of our project.

The fourth thing we are attempting to do is to develop activities for the Indian children who run the streets. Many Indian children stay at home with their families and do not really need the kind of support that we can give them, or perhaps their parents are already giving them that kind of support. But there are other children in the community who do not have that kind of support at home and who need it from some other source. We try to provide it by getting them involved in character-building projects like the Y program, scouting, and 4-H. That requires a lot of coordination with the district community services. It is frustrating trying to set up these projects because the community agencies also need financial support for what they are trying to do and yet our dollars limit what we can do. So we have to sit down and negotiate with them to get Indian children into those programs. In essence this is what our project is about.

We are trying to make this project go in our community. We do not have the kind of discouragement and heartache that I see other people confronted with; we are making things happen, because we are doing these things from the Indian perspective.

I said earlier that before 1965 all my Indian culture came through watching Tonto and Lone Ranger on television. A lot of educators I deal with come from that perspective. They like to think about Indians being the way Tonto was. There is a basic problem in that, which I know because I ran into the reality of being an Indian.

I learned when I was a kid that whenever the Lone Ranger wanted to know something, he asked Tonto. Tonto would put his ear to the railroad track . . . and say, "There's a Union Pacific freight train 3,231 yards down the track, it's got an engine and coal car, 14 boxcars, three flatcars, caboose, a White man is the engineer, Black man is shoveling coal, Chinese man is the conductor."

I used to believe all that until I went back to the reservation and was walking up the road. There was an Indian man lying there, so I went up to him. He looked up and said, "1957 Pontiac, young woman driving, two kids in the back seat." I said, "Can you really tell all that by just listening to the road?" He said, "No, I'm trying to tell you they just ran over me!"

9 Educated or Indian?

(Either/Or)

OWANA MCLESTER-GREENFIELD

As Native American Coordinator for Drake University, Des Moines Area Community College, and Grandview College, Owana McLester-Greenfield, Shoshone, traveled around the state of Iowa listening and talking to Indian students and encouraging them to pursue further education or training after high school. She describes her experiences this way: "Having conceptualized, organized, and set into action what I considered to be an effective program for recruiting, enrolling, and retaining Native Americans, I passed, during the year, from initial stages of optimism and idealism, through disillusionment and near-despair, to, ultimately, a realistic pessimism concerning the Des Moines program and others like it throughout Iowa. The result of that year of emotional and intellectual change is the following chapter." The frustration the author feels reflects her experiences as an Indian within an educational system in which many American Indians prefer not to participate.

The White man does not understand the Indian for the reason that he does not understand America. He is too far removed from its formative processes. The roots of the tree of his life have not yet grasped the rock and soil. The White man is still troubled with primitive fears; he still has in his consciousness the perils of this frontier continent, some of its vastness not yet having yielded to his questing footsteps and inquiring eyes. He shudders still with the memory of the loss of his forefathers upon its scorching deserts and forbidding mountaintops. The man from Europe is still a foreigner and an alien. And he still hates the man who questioned his path across the continent. But in the Indian the spirit of the land is still vested; it will be until other men are able to divine and meet its rhythm. Men must be born and reborn to belong. Their bodies must be formed of the dust of their forefather's bones.
— Luther Standing Bear, Oglala Sioux

After decades of the tragedy — travesty — of less-than-feeble, less-than-half-hearted attempts at the education of the long-neglected, always inhumanly treated American Indian, altruism (some of it insincerely faddish) or coercion has resulted in more and more intensive educational programs for this minority. The best of these programs have been initiated for the higher education of Indians — initiated at the junior college, college, and university levels. The state of Iowa has followed other states throughout the country, imitated, borrowed, and adapted programs designed to better and further the education of the Iowan American Indians. In the recent past, a large number of the universities, private colleges, and junior colleges in Iowa have focused upon the educational deficiencies of the Indian student and undertaken new ventures to eradicate these deficiencies.

Because of the unique features of individual endeavors throughout the state, it would be an arduous task to adequately describe and attempt to do justice to any of these new programs. Therefore, for the sake of necessary brevity, I will try, as nearly as possible, to set forth the main points of a "typical" program, to give a fairly accurate representation of the methods and objectives of these attempts.

It can safely be said that all the new ventures hold recruitment of Indians as the top priority. Students are usually sought from among senior year high school students in the college or university's immediate vicinity. In some cases, the task of recruitment has been assigned to admissions counselors. In others, a recruiter of Indian heritage has been employed to initiate, organize, and administer the program. In such cases, recruitment naturally falls into his or her hands.

A major task of the director of the Native American program is to provide information concerning financial aid for Indian students and explore possible financial assistance sources such as tribal, federal, and scholarship agencies. The same person or persons will assume responsibility for assisting in other necessary areas — perhaps lessen the red tape of admission procedures, help solve housing problems, answer academic questions, or organize an Indian cultural center, should one be desired.

After the initial admission/registration/settling process has been completed, the director may be responsible for personal and academic counseling of Indian students admitted. In addition, he or she may work with the faculty and academic administration to set up American Indian studies programs for the particular college or university.

Such programs as these are vital and have been long awaited and long needed. The goals of those who have finally "come to the aid" of the Native American in Iowa are admirable: to make accessible to the Iowa Indian the level of education the non-Indian in Iowa has been receiving for decades; to get and keep the Iowa Indian student in higher education in Iowa. I believe, however, that all these now-existing programs are doomed to failure unless those who initiate, organize, and operate them become aware of the tremendous obstacles that have prevented the education of Indians in this state throughout past years. These programs are not designed to ameliorate or even deal with the real, underlying problems concerning Indian education. Intentions may be good; these programs may be steps in the right direction. But they are only steps, and they are steps that are in many cases misguided and grossly misdirected. As has happened for years upon years in the past, the same mistakes will be made for the simple reason that those who attempt to provide education for the Indian are ignorant of the attitudes of those for whom that education is designed. They do not know with whom or with what they are dealing.

Yet it is difficult to describe the Indian students with whom educators around the state are dealing, for they vary from area to area; they vary with environment, percentage of Indian heritage, and personal and family attitudes toward this heritage. Some Indians, as many of those from Tama, are fully Indian in appearance, in background, and in cultural heritage. At the opposite extreme, some have become almost, if not completely, assimilated into the White culture and are Indian only by virtue of being born so. These of the second group are not a problem for people concerned with Indian education for, as they have come to identify with the non-Indian way of life, they have also come to adopt White attitudes and life-styles. Indians in the center of these opposite poles form the largest group. Of 50 percent or less Indian blood, they can and often do pass for non-Indian in appearance yet are, at the same time, tied to Indian religious and cultural beliefs inherited from parents and grandparents. They are totally at home in neither the Indian or non-Indian world and identify with only parts of each.

Iowa cannot offer an example of a "typical" Indian. It is not possible to stereotype to facilitate an examination of problems common to all three groups. For purposes of this chapter, the Indian student who has, for all practical purposes, become totally enmeshed in the non-Indian culture will be ignored. This Indian can, for the most part, be considered as a White student with a similar economic environment. Educational problems for him or her will be nearly the same as for most other students in Iowa today, and educational attitudes will be quite similar. It is with the two remaining groups that those who are interested in Indian education must concern themselves. Problems to be dealt with regarding these two groups run in similar veins, although they are naturally more intense for the Indian student who lives fully as an Indian.

Perhaps the gravest mistake made in efforts to educate the Native Americans in this state indirectly relates to the "classification" problem just discussed. The vast majority of the programs in Iowa are set up and functioning at the college, junior college, and university levels. The fingers of these operations reach and pluck from the upper levels of high school. Unfortunately, at the high school level, most of those students who remain are those who have adopted for themselves the White culture. The Indian students who retain their own heritage have long since become disillusioned and disgusted dropouts. It is not an exaggeration to say that most will quit school at the earliest possible chance. The few who do remain in school until graduation time attend sporadically and then because they are forced to. These will not go on for higher education regardless of the number of recruiters who visit them, regardless of the glowing tuition-free promises that are waved in their faces. Reasons for this are many and varied, and will be discussed later.

Those Indians who remain in high school are, as mentioned above, those who can live well in the White environment, who have accustomed themselves to non-Indian living, and who have absorbed White attitudes toward education. They have motivation and desire to learn, have had no particularly unpleasant time in school, and would probably go on to higher levels of education without the aid of Native American programs. The Indian students whom the magic recruiting fingers will ultimately grasp and drop into the college setting are those who, like their non-Indian counterparts, would probably arrive there anyway; their way is only made less difficult. Our new programs are picking from only a small, small minority of Indian students, or could-be Indian students. We have missed and are continuing to miss those who do not remain in school long enough to be helped, those who truly do need the aid these programs are created to provide. We miss them because these Indian students have long since become ex-students. The Indian aiders should be exercising their fingers long before senior high school, during elementary and junior high grades. It is, I believe, more than possible that these students, destined to fail educationally before given the chance to succeed, could be motivated, encouraged, and helped if only they could be reached in time and at the time when they most need assistance.

Because the parents of an Indian child play a crucial role in determining what that student does or becomes and exert a profound influence on the views of their child, their position on education must be understood and evaluated. Views that have existed and have been inherited through the years must be examined, for they have, in many ways, decided the status of Indian education today.

Most students who go on to college are carrying on a tradition that has passed from one generation to another; they have grown up expecting to do so because mother, father, and grandparents did so. There is seldom doubt that they will receive some kind of further educational training; in other words, they have been educationally reinforced throughout the years. In most case, this is not true for the Indian student. There is a conspicuous lack of educational reinforcement from the home. The reason for this is obvious. Pathetically few parents of Indian students today have college degrees; a majority of them do not possess high school diplomas. There is no tradition of college or university graduation to pass on to their children. Education in the past has been for the White man, not for the Indian. It was an impossibility; it was never considered. What little today's parents know of Indian education is discouraging, for past attempts at it have almost always been complete failures. And it is difficult, almost impossible, to begin to change years of inherited views. It will be a major task for those who wish to reach Indian students of today to also reach Indian parents of today, to convince them that education for their children is more than possible, is more and more necessary, for the parents play a major role in determining whether or not their children go on to school. The encouragement, the motivation, must come from them. A tradition of education for Indians must be instilled in them, must be passed on through parents to children, or it will never come about.

How educators will foster this feeling in Indians will be a monumental task, for the Native Americans have tragically few examples to follow and emulate. Educational success stories among them are nearly nonexistent. One can point to few American Indians who have "made good" via the educational process. There are few examples Indian parents can point to and say, "Education will allow my child to do this, to become this." How many doctors, lawyers, politicians, engineers, scientists, business presidents, or store managers of Indian heritage can be found in the United States? Few. Pathetically few. These positions seem to have been reserved throughout the years for the White man. The Indian seems to have been destined to do only menial labor, factory work. If they *chose* such vocations voluntarily, if they truly desired to work for a lifetime in such capacities, we would have another story. But Indians have believed and continue to believe that the lowest caliber of jobs are the only ones they are able to assume. Attitudes must change, both White and Indian. Indian parents and students must be made aware that higher level positions, prestigious positions, challenging and ennobling positions can be shared by the American Indian. Yet there is nothing in our history and in modern society to verify this. This, therefore, must be the starting point. I was deeply saddened to find that students with whom I have talked all over the state intend to work in garages or in factories not because they *want* to but because they believe they cannot do otherwise, that there are no alternatives for them, that they have no choice but to do what their fathers and mothers have done. It is no longer true, but no amount of talking will convince either the Indian parents or their children until they have examples to follow, until they can point to other members in their culture who *prove* that it is no longer true.

Most Indian children in Iowa today come from poor families, many of them poverty-level families. For this reason alone, college is never considered a possibility, is, in fact, never considered at all. To further compound the issue, a large number of Native American students come from one-parent families, families that may have five, six, seven, sometimes eight or nine brothers and sisters living at home. In many cases, the supporting parent is a mother who works full time and who is barely able to maintain her family on an inadequate salary supplemented by financial assistance such as ADC. Children, as they grow older, are expected to assume their share of the financial burden to keep the family clothed and fed. This is never questioned, and for this reason many Indian students quit school as soon as they are old enough to obtain a job of any kind. Having once dropped out and begun working, they seldom, almost never, consider going back to get the high school diploma they were forced to forego because of sheer family need.

The above-mentioned problems are those related to inherited traditions and economic deterrents. Of themselves, they will prevent Indian students in Iowa from participating in high school graduation ceremonies, will prevent Indian students from moving into college residence halls. But, aside from these, there are other equally decisive factors. Other deterrents to Indian education lie with the students themselves in their own attitudes toward education.

In my many, many discussions with Indian students of the two types with which I am concerned, I found few, perhaps none, who admitted to truly enjoying school. Most, if not planning to quit, wanted to. The reasons they offered for doing so were valid. The school environment for Indians is unpleasant, if not unbearable, a great deal of the time. They avail themselves of every opportunity to escape it. Few want to prolong it by going into another similar, though higher-level, environment.

Indian students have immense difficulty in fitting in, adjusting to Iowa school systems, which are almost entirely White in composition. They are, by virtue of appearance and beliefs, "different." They are a conspicuous minority (and what minority is not?). They are usually ostracized, ridiculed. If not, they are quietly ignored. Unless the situation is as it is in Tama, where the Indian students can form a group by themselves, they are often loners. The school atmosphere for the Indian is not the same as for the non-Indian. School days for Indian students are not filled with the excitement of running for class office, of being a cheerleader, of attending the junior prom. Indian students are not among the "social elite" of the high school ranks, nor do they have a peer group with which to identify. The high school classroom for them becomes an alien and often hostile world, which they would escape if they could, will escape when they can, to find security within the family. Few Indian students find enjoyment in school, and few will go on to other schools where they believe, and probably with justification, that it will not be any different.

Exclusion by prejudice from peers certainly determines Indian attitudes toward school and education. These views are further reinforced by prejudice, although many times of a different sort, from teachers, counselors, and principals. Although educators and administrators like to believe, perhaps have convinced themselves, that the enlightened imparters of knowledge working in school systems in Iowa are free from racial prejudice, it simply is not so. Racism exists. In some schools it is covert. In other schools it is blatant. In either case, it manifests itself in various ways.

There are educators in Iowa who are overtly racists. By their own admission they would rather not teach Indian students, who are "dumb" and "lazy" at the very least. The students are condemned as poor students before ever having an opportunity to prove that they are not. As a result, Indian students give up; they feel that they simply cannot win. The negative attitude of some teachers is more than obvious to the Indian students and equally as obvious to the non-Indian students, who are quick to pick it up and incorporate it into their own way of thinking.

On the other hand, there are also educators in Iowa who are so afraid of being charged with discrimination, so afraid of being termed racist, that they completely reverse the process and carry their treatment of Indian students to the opposite extreme. These instructors make fewer demands on their Indian students, allow them to get by with doing less work than non-Indian students, and give the same grade to Indian students as to non-Indian students for work of much poorer quality. Their treatment also damages Indian students who will take advantage of it, who will get little out of their education because they are allowed to put very little into it. This kind of discrimination results in ill-feeling, often bitter resentment, on the part of non-Indian students in the classroom, and the conflict between the two groups is furthered.

These two examples are, of course, the extremes of attitudes and treatment characteristic of teachers in our schools. The majority of educators lie in the middle group, which displays not so much overt prejudice as overt ignorance. Most teachers simply do not understand their Native American students, are ignorant of their backgrounds, their heritage, their life-styles, their beliefs. They do not understand the people with whom they are dealing every day, and they cannot effectively deal with people about whom they know little, if anything. On innumerable occasions I have heard from teachers, counselors, and principals that their Indian students are "so quiet," "so unresponsive in class," or "so aloof from all the other students." They assume the reason for this is that Indian students are either dumb or feel superior to their White classmates. Indian students are sadly misunderstood, and teachers of Indian students are sadly misinformed.

Few educators understand that part of the Indian student's lack of enthusiasm for doing class assignments or for participating in class discussions stems from the fact that, almost without exception, what the Indian student is forced to learn is White, deals with White culture, White history, White literature. What is offered in Iowa schools is a White education, and although ours is a White country for the most part, what is Indian is important to the Indian. And what is truly Indian is not incorporated into what is taught in schools. Because of this, it is unrealistic to expect that an Indian student will be totally absorbed in what goes on in the Iowa classroom today. Indian students have told me that on the few occasions (which are, however, becoming more frequent) when Indian literature or culture is discussed, they are called upon to "explain what it's like to be Indian." The "class Indian" approach is devastating, for no Indian can explain "Indianness"; it cannot be learned in an hour or a week, and it cannot, at any time, be comprehended by those who know nothing about it. An Indian student's attempts to explain only serve to make him or her more conspicuous, more different, and, therefore, more alienated.

The damaging effect of being an outsider, being subjected to ridicule and exclusion, cannot be minimized. It will take a great toll. And, should the more able, more highly motivated Indian students be able to endure the unpleasantness (often anguish) of "differentness" throughout their years in high school, they will find a way to obtain further education without further ostracism. The greatest share of those few who go on to institutions of higher learning will not remain in Iowa. They will go to the Haskells and Bacones; it is unreasonable to think they will not. An Indian student who has suffered through years of prejudice will not willingly submit to more. He or she will not voluntarily become again an Indian on a White campus; and Iowa campuses are White. The small number who want further training, who, miraculously enough, have found the encouragement and motivation, will go to Indian schools that can offer the peer group security that schools in Iowa cannot. They will go on to Indian schools where they can identify with, live and learn with, share with students of similar cultural backgrounds and beliefs. One or two Indian recruiters, one or two Indian faculty members, do not an Indian school make. Our Native Americans will go to schools where faculty and staff (and students) know them and understand them.

These, then, are the real issues concerning Indian education as I see them, as I have been made to realize them by Indian students in school in Iowa today. Unfortunately, there are other problems, many other problems (for example, how can the Indian student who does not live on Indian-owned land receive the federal aid to which he or she should be entitled?). The matters considered in this chapter are, I believe, those needing the most urgent attention. These problems must be dealt with if any progress is ever to be made in the area of Indian education. Those who are organizing and operating educational programs for Indian students must become aware of them, must search for solutions to them. They must rethink their approaches, examine their directions, begin to understand the people with whom they are dealing and the attitudes, inherited and learned, of those people. Until this is done, until the real problems are solved, or at least alleviated, our Indian students will remain uneducated. We simply have not fostered an atmosphere that will allow them to be both Indian and educated.

10   Education, the Family, and the Schools

ADELINE WANATEE

As a student, Adeline Wanatee was forbidden to speak her native Mesquakie language. As a grandmother, she saw that the language survived despite the great odds, and with the language the culture of her people endures. Her concern, however, prompted her to initiate weekly language classes so that young Mesquakie as well as some non-Indians could study the written language of the tribe. Although most Mesquakie children speak their own language before English, most of them never learn to write it and, in fact, risk losing it if they leave the community. Her concern, outlined in this chapter, was the effect of the educational systems on Indian children — what must they give up to become "educated"? Extensive research in the area of Indian education indicates that there are negative, even hostile, views held by American Indians toward educational institutions. Through cooperative programs that include Indian people in the planning and implementation, schools can begin to reflect the pluralistic society in which we all live.

. . . *many schools for Indian children make them ashamed they are Indians. . . . The schools forget these are Indian children. They don't recognize them as Indians, but treat them as though they were white children. . . . This makes for failure, because it makes for confusion. And when the Indian history and the Indian culture is ignored, it makes our children ashamed they are Indians.*
— *Ben Black Elk, Sioux*

As a woman and a mother as well as a grandmother, I am especially concerned about the educational process that affects the Indian child in school as well as in the family and the community. All education ultimately superimposes "culture" on the young. However formal or informal, the process of education is dependent on how children are taught and the ultimate role the women play in this learning experience.

We have always talked about the dominant culture imposing upon the minorities — the Anglo-oriented, urban/industrial culture with all its technological skills and know-how bringing automatic relief to all the ills of mankind. And, where the Indian people are involved, the Anglo-controlled schools, the Bureau of Indian Affairs schools, and the missionary and public schools have all openly and consistently sought to destroy the native tribal cultures and tried to impose the Anglo culture. In this effort they have failed, and they have helped me to understand what my role is in the educational process of the child within the Indian community.

I, as a woman not too different from my ancestors, have the tremendous job of bringing this seemingly destructive course around to where the educational system will involve not only the school but also the community, the parents, and the students in a learning process beneficial to our children.

I know what "acculturation" (assimilation and elimination) is like: it is the continuing common denominator of a policy toward the Indian people to remove them from their heritages and cultures. A physical genocide was attempted, then removal to the "Far West" was completed; the only thing left was the cultural genocide and that had moderate success among many tribes. By an estimate given by John Collier, Franklin D. Roosevelt's Commissioner of Indian Affairs, over 75 million Indian people were killed in the Americas from 1500 to 1900, and many also died and were afflicted by the diseases brought here by the immigrants. Next, the forced removal of all Indian people to the remote places in the West brought many trails-of-tears and broken families; the Dawes Severalty Act of the late 1880s reduced Indian Lands (reservations) from 150 million acres to less than one-third that amount, thereby effectively destroying the community-tribal structures of many groups. Then the emphasis was shifted from physical genocide to cultural genocide: schools of all sorts were established in an all-out effort to stamp out the old ways. "Trade schools" and BIA, missionary, and state schools were all used as a means to an end: wipe out the languages and you will do away with the means of transmitting a culture, therefore, doing away with a people. In the early 1900s, Indian leaders were being wooed and courted in the halls of Congress in Washington, D.C., and many went home broken and without people to lead; the process of purchasing rights was at a maximum and the Indian people unknowingly paid dearly. In 1924 the Indian was declared a "citizen" by an act of Congress, but for that right he was expected to disregard his culture and become like everybody else. He was told to forget about his culture as it produces useless and idle things like corn, beans, and squash. Letters from the commissioner to each tribe suggested that the Indian "pow wows" too much, neglecting his livestock, his family, or his home.

How did these events affect the Indian community structure? Many tribes had matrilineal structures to hold the community together, and the League of Six Nations was governed by women. Some Indian tribes gave the women dual roles whenever feasible — as the "property owner" and as a "tribal-council member." We have had, since the 1934 Indian Reorganization Act, an article in the Mesquakie Tribal Constitution and Bylaws giving women the right to positions on the council. Today, we still adhere to the old ways, but we are having a difficult time. While non-Indians are still fighting over what color, what sex, or how much money or wealth they possess, we are gradually losing our riches through our youth because of the impositions and superimpositions placed on our culture. My role as a "minority woman" becomes doubly important as I am able to direct and control what my children and grandchildren will learn, both in the White man's and Indian's educational processes. Indian cultures do not generally lay stress on competition and conflict geared toward materialistic things; however, we find it increasingly important to learn how to become well educated to sustain ourselves and our culture. Each individual or group of individuals has its own uniqueness and each is incredibly complex — especially from the non-tangible philosophical-theological standpoint. The only way a culture can be measured is to measure its ideals against its realities. Indian cultures lay a heavy emphasis on the ancient principle of tribal responsibility; hence, the individual has an obligation to the tribe and, in return, the group or tribe is obliged and responsible to the individual. Without this system the circle is broken and the balance between communal cooperation and the individual/family autonomy is lost. The child looks elsewhere for a culture. I am still trying to impose my culture on my children and will always instruct our young in the more specific and general components of tribal culture and ways.

But, non-Indians have within their grasp the means to superimpose their cultural ways and sometimes essential technological advances; in the past two hundred years especially, the school, a formal western institution replete with laws and customs, has added to my difficulties in the upbringing of my children. When the men of the tribe have lost their status as the instructors of the young and are denied many other responsibilities in the raising of their children, when Anglo-controlled and Anglo-oriented schools seek to destroy the traditional cultures we value, and when the Indian students find themselves enmeshed in the most negative learning situation, the student begins early in life to differentiate between the two cultures. This can be helpful and meaningful to the individual, but it can harm the community. In its final form, at best, the school that caters to the European cultures and histories and says little or nothing of an honest or objective nature about the Native or other non-White minority peoples superimposes upon my role as an "educator" and "provider" for my own people. I think that to have a vital role in the minority situation, whether in education, family, economics, politics, or culture, I need to look at the public school as an openly negative and dangerous institution. It directly interferes with the educational process of our Indian youth; it is psychologically injurious to the Indian and other non-White students in a racist/ethnocentric fashion; and it is directly and psychologically injurious to White students. This is contrary to what I was taught, and one of our most basic commitments to all the young people is to the complex relationships and interrelationships encompassing the student, parent, family, and the school. Hence, where Indian people exist in numbers, there is a growing insistence for Indian control of the schools, teaching the culture through history, language, and music. After two hundred years, the Indian people today deserve a place in the educational universe. We need Indian administrators, teachers, counselors, historians, spiritual leaders, and medicine men; here the curriculum format grows directly out of the cultural values of the community and into the non-Indian curriculum dimensions of the technological world. This use of Indian personnel must take place soon or the imposition of an alien culture will continue, either through commission or omission.

The National Indian Education Association has indicated several priorities regarding Indian education: the development of curricular materials relevant to Indian youth; the presentation of the historical and social truths in the classrooms; the use of textbooks dealing honorably with the Indians; the training and instructing of Indian teachers to approach the Indian student in the bicultural and bilingual setting; and the involvement of Indian parents and the community in the decision-making process, thereby reinforcing the role of the parents in the education of Indian youth.

In the coming year you will see as you look across the sky and heavens a faint light. As you listen for the sound, only a whisper will you hear, but the effect of its passing within the universe will bring about many changes in your lives as well as ours.

11 The American Indian in Sioux City

A Historical Overview

MICHAEL HUSBAND

& GARY KOERSELMAN

In this chapter the authors review Sioux City's past and make several positive suggestions for the classroom teacher who is teaching both Indian and non-Indian students in the present.

Again, and maybe the last time on earth, I recall the great vision you sent me. It may be that some little root of the sacred tree still lives. Nourish it, then, that it may leaf and bloom and fill with singing birds. Hear me, not for myself but for my people; I am old. Hear me, that they may once more go back into the sacred hoop and find the good road and the shielding tree.

— Black Elk, Oglala Sioux

Sioux City, located in western Iowa on the banks of the Missouri River, took its name from the Sioux River and originally from the American Indian tribe of the same name. The community has an Indian population composed of many tribal groups, although the largest number are members of the Santee Sioux, Winnebago, and Omaha tribes. The city has long attracted area Indian people seeking opportunities for improved social and economic conditions. The 1970 census lists the total population of the Sioux City metropolitan area as 116,109 and the Indian population as 865. The latter figure is probably low; other estimates place the number as high as 1,700.

The Omaha people, having moved from the eastern United States, came in contact with some of the earliest fur traders operating in and around Council Bluffs and Bellevue. By 1804, when Lewis and Clark came through the area, the Omaha were living at Ton-won-ton-ga — "the big village" — near Homer, Nebraska, about twenty miles south of Sioux City. The Omaha Reservation, located south of Sioux City in what is now Thurston County, Nebraska, was established by the treaty of March 16, 1854, which provided for a cession of 93 million acres to the United States. By a subsequent treaty of March 6, 1865, the Omaha transferred the northern half of their reservation to the Winnebago tribe. Alice Fletcher and Francis La Flesche, in their classic study of the Omaha people, note that sorghum and corn were harvested in the winter by the Omaha, and the produce was hauled on the ice to the "new settlement" of Sioux City more than a century ago.

The Winnebago tribe lived in the Green Bay and Lake Winnebago areas of Wisconsin when the Europeans arrived on the North American continent. The tribe ceded millions of acres of aboriginal land before being moved to Iowa and Minnesota and then to South Dakota. The Nebraska Winnebago, comprising about 1,200 people, were settled near the Omaha people in 1865, and in March of that year the treaty establishing the Winnebago reservation was negotiated.

The Santee Sioux moved to their present reservation near Niobrara, Nebraska, in 1866. Following the White-Indian conflicts in Minnesota in 1862, the Santee had been removed to Crow Creek, South Dakota, and thence to their present Nebraska reservation.

Sioux City was incorporated by legislative act on January 16, 1857. The Dakota Sioux were frequent visitors to the city, and although Iowa became a state in 1848, northwest Iowa was still possessed and occupied by Indian people in the mid-nineteenth century. Sioux City was situated on the borderland between the new area of settlement and the Indian lands, and the town became a "jumping-off" point for the far western frontier. One of the city's earliest settlers, a French trader named Theophile Brughier, who was a native of Canada and who had been in the employ of the American Fur Company, had married a daughter of the legendary Sioux Chief War Eagle. It was the chief, in fact, who assisted Brughier in finding a suitable spot for a farm and trading post at the mouth of the Big Sioux River, about two miles above Sioux City, in 1849. Brughier's Post became a gathering spot for area Indians and headquarters for French trading activities in the region. War Eagle died in 1851 and is buried on the lofty bluff near the mouth of the Big Sioux River overlooking three states. Planning for the development of a park and cultural center at the site of his grave is currently in progress.

Transcultural relations of a less cordial nature also characterized early contacts between Sioux Cityans and area Indian tribes. The Sioux City Frontier Guards, for example, were a home company established in 1861, and the group was reflective of increasing tensions between the Indian and White communities at that time. The force of westward expansion, coupled with the withdrawal of regular troops from the Missouri River garrisons above Sioux City and the disturbances in Minnesota in 1862, led to conflicts among the Sioux and non-Indian residents along the Floyd and Little Sioux rivers, although the guards did not see heavy fighting. The Sioux City Cavalry, which operated as an independent military organization from the fall of 1861 until early 1863, was stationed in squads at various points, including Spirit Lake, Cherokee, and Correctionville.

Like other urban Indian populations, Sioux City's Indian people and their needs, dreams, and goals have been frequently misunderstood, and the transition from reservation to urban life has been, in many instances, a traumatic experience both socially and economically. Benny Bearskin, a Winnebago Indian, speaks of the problems and promises associated with "getting urbanized":

> Getting urbanized. I like this term. It means you have to learn the ropes, just like a person moving out from the prairie country into the woods. You know, there are certain dangers in such a transition, and it's the same way in a city. Yes, you have to learn the ropes. And once you become urbanized, this means to me that you're gonna settle down, and you have to have a goal to look forward to. Otherwise, I think it would drive you crazy. . . .
>
> Four of our children were born here in this city, and yet, I think, they're oriented as American Indians. I make it a point to take them on my vacation trips in the summer, always to a different reservation to get acquainted with the people of the tribe. We take photographs, we record the songs that are sung, we participate in dancing and compete for prizes. . . .
>
> I think those Indians who retain the greatest amount of their cultural heritage are really very fortunate, because they feel that it's more important to retain one's dignity and integrity and go through life in this manner, than spending all their energy on the accumulation of material wealth. They find this a frustrating situation. I think the Indian is the only nationality under the system who has resisted this melting-pot concept. Everybody else wants to jump in, they view this idea, jumping in and becoming American or losing identity. . . .
>
> It's so impersonal. I think this makes itself felt in many situations. For instance, when you become urbanized, you learn how to think in abstract terms. Now when you get here on Broadway, to catch a CTA bus going south, you subconsciously know there's a driver, but you take no interest in him at all as a person, he's more

like an object. And it's the same way in schools. The teacher is there to do a certain function. And I think the teacher also feels that these pupils are like a bunch of bumps on a log. You know, this can be a difficult thing, especially for an Indian child, who, in his family life, learns to establish relationships on a person-to-person basis. And he finds that this is absent in the classroom. And frequently parents go to talk to the principal, to talk to the teacher; it's just like going over there talking to a brick wall. They feel you just aren't hip. Something is wrong with you, and if you don't conform, it's just too bad. . . .

Poverty is not merely the lack of wealth, a lack of money. It goes much deeper than that. There's poverty in reservations and where there are no reservations, and where there are no Indians. What we try to do here, at the Center (American Indian Center) is to some way, somehow, get people *involved*. Most of these people are coping with their problems on a day-to-day basis. The future is something that rarely enters their minds.

I think there will be some radical changes taking place. We have a younger generation, in the age bracket of my oldest daughter. I think in the future Indians will make a bigger contribution. It's been pointed out that Indians should feel that if it was not for the land which they owned, this would not be the greatest nation on earth. . . .[1]

Although Bearskin speaks of his experiences in Chicago, urban Indian people as a whole face similar difficulties and prospects in cities, including the problem of the availability of federal services to urban Indians, and housing, employment, educational, and identity problems characteristic of city life. John W. Olson, an Assiniboine Indian and a social casework director at the Chicago American Indian Center, speaks to the educational and identity problems as they apply to many urban Indian people in various American cities:

A minimum level of educational preparedness seems to be essential for a successful move to the city. A person must be able to speak and write an acceptable form of noncolloquial English grammar. The problem no longer is that the Indians speak their own language instead of English, but rather that they lack adequate training in acceptable English. In addition, there are certain skills that constitute minimal conditions for steady employment. It is impossible to separate the problems of education and employment; they are intertwined.

Added to the educational and occupational problems are the numerous psychological components of the human personality. Problems of identity and awareness of self, of purpose, of realistic means to desirable ends, of flexible attitudes — trying to solve the problems as they occur rather than trying to predict and prevent them. We have good intentions, but the truth is that we still do not know enough. However, we believe that the decisions should be made by Indians, not by others. Other people have attempted to make our lives for us; now it is time for us to take an active rather than passive role in Indian directions.[2]

These and other socioeconomic factors have directly affected Indian students in the Sioux City public schools. Indeed, at the beginning of the seventies, the school dropout rate among the system's nearly 300 Indian students (more than 50 percent of Iowa's American Indian students attend school in two districts: Sioux City and the South Tama County Schools) hovered around the 100 percent mark. In response to this situation, Morningside College sponsored, during the 1973–74 academic year, an Indian Studies Institute, funded under Title IV of the 1964 Civil Rights Act.

The project involved more than twenty teachers from schools with a significant Indian population in an attempt to expand teacher awareness and to develop means by which Indian students could be encouraged to remain in school until graduation, thus acquiring the skills necessary to help adapt to urban life, to gain desirable employment, and to provide leadership for their people.

The first phase involved the participants in a careful self-study of the instructional materials and other pertinent conditions affecting the Indian students in their particular teaching situation and the second phase involved the participants in a highly concentrated summer institute at Morningside College.

Participants in the program were reminded of the importance of a sound knowledge of the Indian historical experience on both the national and regional levels. Local Indian representatives discussed their experiences as Indians growing up in Sioux City and/or on nearby reservations. They also compared and contrasted the dominant Indian and non-Indian cultural values and discussed the importance of maintaining a positive Indian identity in schooling situations historically saturated by White cultural ways. The following incident, related by a Sioux City school counselor, emphasizes a recurring problem stemming, in part, from traditional curricular inadequacies:

I asked an Indian boy who came to school if he was from Santee. He answered, "No, I think I'm Omaha." This Indian boy had uncertainties about his tribal affiliation. There are many like this who are in urban schools. This boy has forgotten his culture and heritage. The children should have a knowledge of their Indian heritage. We visit the homes where they live. Teachers and other people who have anything to do with Indian education must see if these people are making it. Where they reside is not the choice of the child so we have to meet his needs wherever he resides. I think there is a definite problem when the student represents two minorities. It is not that kid's fault. The urban student makes a culture of his own. The people are fragmented. There is some apathy toward the urban child. The Indian kids in the urban situation do not have the curriculum — more needs to be done to meet this type of need. I would like to get some ideas. I think a special education team should be developed to go into urban areas to get this worked out. Each State should have a team — this State does not. One program that I think is good for urban school systems is the program founded for workshops to promote an awareness about Indian people and to develop some related material. We have a program operating like this in Sioux City.[3]

The institute provided participants with new ideas for improving the educational experiences of both Indian students and, in the final analysis, *all* students. Indian and non-Indian consultants demonstrated how teachers could enhance their success in the classroom by taking account of the Indian world view, Indian models of human success, Indian methods of solving personal problems, the function of the "teacher" as perceived by Indian culture, career awareness, and parental involvement.

The use of Winnebago, Omaha, and Sioux tribal stories in the school curriculum was proposed, and the oral history process, as a legitimate teaching-learning tool, was emphasized. Oral history, that is, the collection (through interviewing), the transcribing, and the utilization of oral testimony, can be a valuable teaching tool as one attempts to project to students the history and culture of a people who did not record their history in the traditional Western documentary style. The oral history process, when used in conjunction with the printed sources that exist, can give students a more balanced and certainly a more vivid and honest picture of Indian culture.

By the end of the summer institute participants had developed "plans of action" designed to foster significant changes in their respective schools. The participants implemented their plans during the 1973–74 academic school year. Staff closely monitored the activities through classroom visitations, individual conferences, conference sharing days, and a follow-up session in June 1974. Several of the plans of action helped to achieve the project's main purpose of helping Indian students stay in school through enhanced identification with the educational process. The plans received a great amount of assistance from local Indian representatives who came into classrooms as resource persons to teach Indian crafts, history, and culture. Several plans called for a special emphasis on Native American history and culture in social studies classes. Some participants assigned oral history projects dealing with the Indian experience in Sioux City. Others invited Indian parents in as teacher's aides. One participant asked her students to read and reply to Chief Sitting Bull's letter to his grandchildren. Another organized an Indian-American club at a high school. Yet another participant taught weaving, beading, and sand painting in art classes.

Plans of action such as those noted above seem to have a positive influence on the performance of Indian students. The new emphasis in many of the classes helped them identify better with the classroom activities and caused White children to better understand, appreciate, and respect Indian ways and the Indian history of the Sioux City region. After one minicourse involving the teaching of Winnebago language and music, an Indian student exclaimed: "That's the best class I *ever* had." His White counterparts heartily agreed.

Others benefited as well. Some Indian parents became more actively involved. Teachers who had not been participants successfully adopted some of the new techniques, and new lines of communication between the Indian and White urban communities were developed. Participants themselves learned more about the problems and increased their commitment toward positive change in the school system, not only for Indians but for all students.

The cooperative efforts of Indian people, teachers, administrators, and the non-Indian public are essential if cross-cultural understanding on the urban level is to be achieved and if some first steps in the "1,000 mile journey" toward a truly unbiased community respectful of individual uniqueness are to be taken. This type of cooperation, encouraged by Sioux City's several active Indian organizations, bodes well for the future of Indian/non-Indian relations in Sioux City.

NOTES

1. Studs Terkel, *Division Street: America* (New York: Avon Books, 1967), pp. 134–42.

2. Jack O. Waddell and Michael Watson, eds., *The American Indian in Urban Society* (Boston: Little, Brown and Co., 1971), pp. 407–8.

3. *Symposium on Indian Education* (Vermillion: The Institute of Indian Studies of the University of South Dakota, 1974), p. 12.

12 The American Indian and Ethnicity in Iowa's Future

JOSEPH HRABA

In this chapter Joseph Hraba brings together the ideas voiced by participants on the panel "Urban and Rural Indians in Iowa" and proposes an Ethnic Commission to foster better understanding among the various ethnic groups in Iowa. The panel was part of the 1974 symposium "Indian Perspectives in Iowa: Education, Spiritual Freedom, and Social Responsibility" sponsored by the United Native American Student Association and the Committee on American Indian Studies of Iowa State University. The panel was introduced by United States Congressman John C. Culver and was made up of the following members: George Barta (Yankton Sioux), American Indian Movement; Ed Cline (Omaha), former chairman of the Omaha tribe and field trainer in Indian education for the Coalition of Indian-Controlled School Boards; Kelcy Packineau (Hidatsa and Sioux), American Indian Development Center Board; Charles Pushetonequa (Mesquakie), Sac and Fox Tribal Council; Reuben Snake (Winnebago), National American Indian Leadership Training Program; Pete Stanislaw (Flathead), Cedar Rapids; Aaron Two Elk (Ogalala Sioux), American Indian Movement; J. Adeline Wanatee (Mesquakie), Mesquakie Education Committee; Priscilla Wanatee (Mesquakie), Sac and Fox Housing Authority; Anthony Thomas (Winnebago), Sioux City.

Who will find peace with the lands? The future of mankind lies waiting for those who will come to understand their lives and take up their responsibilities to all living things. Who will listen to the trees, the animals, and birds, the voices of the places of the land? As the long-forgotten peoples of the respective continents rise and begin to reclaim their ancient heritage, they will discover the meaning of the land of their ancestors. That is when the invaders of the North American continent will finally discover that for this land, God is Red.
— Vine Deloria, Jr., Sioux

Let's look ahead. Behind us is a dismal record of Whites neglecting, exploiting, and even attempting to exterminate the American Indian. No longer does the nation believe that "manifest destiny" justifies this record. When Indians came to Iowa State University in the spring of 1974, one might have expected that they would emphasize this horrible past. However, Indian panelists chose instead to look to the future in their discussion.

What is the future for American Indians? No one is certain, of course, but the panelists were emphatic about what they hoped the future would bring American Indians. Naturally they want to improve the material conditions of their lives, yet they feel it is far more important to preserve their ethnicity, their traditions.

To preserve their traditions, and in some instances to restore them, the panelists asked that other Americans first recognize the integrity of the traditional Indian way of life and its communion with the Creator, nature, each other, and the land.

Communion with the Creator was expressed by Mr. Charles Pushetonequa, a Mesquakie council member from Tama, Iowa:

> And you say that we are heathens. I say that we are not. We are more religious than any other race today. We are aware of Him every day, not only on Sundays. Everything we do is done in a religious sort of way.

Religion is not just a separate element of Indian life, for it is woven into the entire fabric of that life. For traditional Indians, this spiritualism is manifest in all things, it animates all life, and it strengthens their communion with nature, with each other, and with the land.

Communion with nature was the focus of a comment made by Mrs. Adeline Wanatee, a Mesquakie, when she was asked how others could better understand the Indian way of life:

> May you increase in the wisdom of the wild, walk many long pleasant trails, and learn to speak with the creatures of the wild.

And in response to the same question, Mr. Pushetonequa reiterated Mrs. Wanatee's sentiments: ". . . the Indian has a lot to offer in our life. You call us people of nature. And everything in life revolves around nature."

It may be informative to some that animism, this spiritualism, also characterized our European ancestors' vision in the Old World:

> Trees, rocks, springs, had also each its appellation, and every day of the year its own designation from the saint or festival that gave it its quality.

> All the objects of nature, being animate, had understanding enough to react to conditions about them. They had a kind of intelligence which while different from man's, was not necessarily inferior.[1]

A communion with nature should not be hard for other Americans to recognize and understand, for it is part of their own heritage as well as that of the Indian.

Indians have a sense of unity with each other, a sense of solidarity that at times transcends individual welfare. Notice this sense of home and unity expressed in a comment by Mr. Cline, an Omaha:

> I think that our sense of values is to share. When we hear the drums a certain time of the year, now today, we come. We don't care — we might have a good job . . . , but when we hear the drums we got to go home.

Along with religion and communion with nature, a sense of belonging to a people is in the fabric of traditional Indian life.

All that is Indian — the spiritualism, communion with nature and with each other — happens on the land. The land is the setting in which Indian life goes on, and where it must be preserved. Loss of land is a point of grievance for Indians because the land provides the geographical base to their cultural survival.

The land is crucial for Indian identity, without it he knows he is dead, and therefore he will die for it:

> There's a mother whose son gave his life in Vietnam, and they sent his body home, and she asked me why did my son die across the water for people, and for what?

> The only thing I said was that many times have our Indian people died for this land, and I'm sure that your son has died for this land, once again, you have died once again for your homelands.

So it was, Indians of Iowa came together in the spring of 1974 to call for mutual understanding, taking the first step by depicting their heritage for us. But, can these traditions be preserved?

THE CHALLENGE

The survival of the traditional Indian way of life is threatened. While the challenge to this heritage comes from several sources, the panelists accentuated how public education and the political process undermine Indian ethnicity.

Too often in the public schools of Iowa, Indian children are expected to learn thoroughly what passes for White culture, but neither they nor White children are instructed in Indian traditions. Indian culture is virtually ignored in public education, while even the Indian children are expected to learn some official version of our national culture, one in which Indians are absent. Either by intent or default public education attempts to corrode the transmission of Indian heritage.

At times public education does far worse than ignore Indian heritage. When this heritage has been presented in public schools, it has occasionally been done in an insensitive and even degrading manner. An Indian child is thereby asked to be ashamed of what he is, and simultaneously non-Indian children are denied a complete education.

By humiliating Indian children or simply ignoring their heritage, public education causes problems for Indian students. They have the highest school dropout rate of any ethnic group in Iowa. This is a disaster, for as George Barta, a panelist from Sioux City, observed, "Education is critical to Indians in facing the political challenge to their survival as a cultural group."

Another threat to Indian heritage lies in the relationship between the Indians of Iowa and government. Several panelists complained about the Bureau of Indian Affairs. Their complaints crystallized into three issues.

First, in the minds of some panelists, the bureau implements in governmental programs an incorrect definition of tribal membership. The result is that Indians unconcerned with traditions share equally with the traditionalists in these programs. This conflict between traditionalists and nontraditionalists is found in nearly all tribes.

The issue of tribal membership is most critical in policies concerning the control and use of Indian land. As would be expected, Indians who have assimilated into the White middle class desire the private ownership of Indian land, for they can thereby sell their shares for liquid capital. Obviously, this results in the erosion of Indian land holdings. This erosion is anathema to more traditional Indians who see land as the center for Indian identity and the only place where Indian culture can be preserved. Consequently, they favor the communal or tribal ownership of land allowing for the strict control of land use and sale in the interests of preserving the tribe as a cultural group.

Second among the conflicts between Indians and the government is that the latter often views Indians as another minority caught in the tangle of poverty, ignorance, disease, and disorganization. Indians do not like this version of themselves as historical victims. Rather they want to be recognized as Indians in terms of their own heritage, not just another minority, and treated as equal citizens in our nation.

Finally and foremost among the issues raised by the panelists was their wish for more Indian control over governmental agencies affecting their lives, whether these agencies are school boards or the Bureau of Indian Affairs. This desire echoes in the rhetoric of many ethnic groups, Blacks and Chicanos as well as Indians. Indians wish to become what sociologists term a corporate group so that they can preserve their way of life. To do so, Indians must increase their economic and political resources and in this way mitigate outside control of Indian affairs.

STRATEGY

But, how is this to be done? Can American Indians preserve their traditional ways in the face of the powerful forces of modernity? I believe the answer is yes. Such questions must never be couched as either/or propositions: ethnic preservation or improvement in material well-being. Rather, it should be asked if both can be done concurrently. We shall now suggest a mechanism by which Indians can simultaneously stimulate their economic and political development and acquire greater control over the survival of their heritage.

Basically Indians must become a corporate group, able to control their internal affairs, define themselves accurately in the public imagery, and most importantly, regulate their exchange with outsiders. Many of the panelists spoke of ways Indians could move in this direction and thereby enhance the material and spiritual life on reservations.

Mrs. Priscilla Wanatee noted a need for better housing for the Sac and Fox. In 1968 a Sac and Fox housing authority was established to meet housing needs, but progress has been less than desirable. She attributes this lack of progress to the fact that Indians do not fully control the housing authority:

I think the reason we're not moving as fast as the people want is that the housing authority was created under the Bureau of Indian Affairs guidelines.

So, our goal now is to set up a program that will fit the needs of the people of the settlement instead of the programs fitting the needs of the Bureau of Indian Affairs guidelines.

Several other panelists spoke for the need to bring education to the reservation and to have such programs under Indian supervision so that Indian needs are served. Adeline Wanatee noted that education is most important in the transmission of Indian heritage from one generation to the next, and to this end she has been active in parent committees on education at the Mesquakie settlement.

Both Mrs. Wanatee and Mr. Cline spoke of their high regard for the efforts of the Coalition of Indian-controlled School Boards. Mr. Cline was also impressed with the cooperation between the Omaha and the University of Nebraska, cooperation that brought college courses to the reservation, which avoided the cultural shock that often accompanies higher education for minorities. Such efforts facilitate the education of American Indians and should improve their competitive posture in the American labor force.

Of course none of these efforts can be successful without the cooperation of the larger society. Indians do not live in pristine isolation any more than any other ethnic group does, and they must rely on some symbiotic exchange with the government and with other people.

Senator John C. Culver of Iowa clearly recognized this fact of Indian life:

> The American Indian doesn't have many votes in the United States. In numerical terms, terms of political power and access, their (Indian) influence is minimal.

But the needs of Indians are great, and Senator Culver cited what he perceives to be some of these needs:

> One (need) is central to any attempt to help the Indian, the necessity to provide for increased control of Indian affairs by Indians . . . (2) expanded programs aimed at directly benefiting the Indian . . . (3) increased health assistance . . . and (4) the Indian must be given the opportunity to develop economic self-sufficiency.

This dilemma of having minimal political clout, coupled with great problems, gives Indians no alternative to cooperating with others. The pressing need is to increase the political power of Indians at the federal and state levels. Mr. Cline cited the establishment of an Indian Commission in Nebraska as a step in that direction. Through that agency, Indians in Nebraska can work with other governmental bureaus as political peers. Such an Indian Commission in Iowa might also be effective, and through this commission, Indians in this state might facilitate their economic and political development and simultaneously realize greater control over their heritage.

ETHNIC COMMISSION

Any state commission mandated to serve the interests of only one ethnic group in Iowa, however, would fall short in two ways. First, while an Indian Commission might help Indians, the efforts of such a commission would continually face opposition, since other ethnic groups would not see their interests being coincidently served. Instead, other groups could become suspicious about state favoritism toward Indians. To the extent that Indians and the rest of Iowa are interdependent, such opposition eventually would retard the progress of Indians in this state. On the other hand, an ethnic commission serving the interests of additional ethnic groups in Iowa would not as likely arouse intergroup suspicions, envy, and antagonism. When mandated to work for many groups, an ethnic commission's efforts on behalf of any one group would more likely be seen by other groups as synchronous with their own interests. In a broader sense, an ethnic commission would provide a forum in which the diverse interests of various ethnic groups could be articulated. It is nearly an axiom in sociological lore that when group conflict is institutionalized, as rules are established to settle differences, conflict measurably decreases.

An Indian Commission would fall short in a second way. Any agency mandated to serve only one ethnic group is unlikely to foster reciprocal understanding among groups with respect to their heritages. More likely, the agency would be parochial and unappreciative of the broad mosaic of ethnic group relations in this state. To diffuse knowledge and thereby understanding of various heritages is a far more imaginative and practical undertaking, and it would be a far better corrective of mutual suspicion and strife. We all need to know more about each other.

As I imagine it, an ethnic commission would have a mandate in both economic and educational affairs relevant to ethnicity in Iowa. As an educator, I would be most interested in the educational services provided through such a commission. But, as a realist, let me first consider the economic services that an ethnic commission could offer.

An ethnic commission could advance the economic interests of Indians as well as other groups through providing information and expertise in securing private and public funding. In this way it would function as a much needed clearinghouse. Securing funding for ethnic groups would facilitate indigenous control over heritage conservation for Indians as well as for others. An ethnic commission could function not only in securing funding but also in facilitating the involvement of ethnic groups in all spheres of state activity. In short, whenever an ethnic group would relate with an outside organization, the ethnic commission would be there to help.

Furthermore, an ethnic commission could help Indians generate income through tourism. Ethnicity has tourist appeal and could be incorporated into recent efforts to bring more tourists to Iowa. Ethnicity could be included in current offerings, in the many artistic, musical, sporting, and historical sites and events in the state. There are many natural areas in Iowa where this could be done. Besides American Indians in central and northwest Iowa, there are Amish in eastern Iowa, Czechs in northeast Iowa, Italians and Blacks in Des Moines, and Scandinavians in central Iowa. These areas could be developed into tourist attractions, and if the groups so desired, resources generated by tourism could apply toward the conservation of their heritage.

For example, the Mesquakie Settlement in Tama County, Iowa, could be developed for more tourist appeal. At this site, tourists could be informed about Sac and Fox heritage in the forms of lessons and illustrative tours in nature lore; lessons and exhibitions on traditional practices in cooking, hunting, and building; lessons on the techniques and meaning of some of the secular rituals; and presentations on the history of the Sac and Fox. The Mesquakie might also consider establishing a summer camp for youth, during which participants would be instructed in Indian heritage.

Such development is possible, provided that an ethnic commission would help with initial investment of capital and management. Furthermore, efforts at Tama could be coordinated through an ethnic commission with tourist development elsewhere in Iowa. Thereby, Iowa would offer tourists several heritages, putting into play a multiplier effect, as each site would attract tourists who would probably visit other sites in the state as well.

With the help of educators and historians, conservation of ethnic authenticity in this effort is within the realm of possibility. If sites at Tama and elsewhere were actually authentic reconstructions of the past, visits to these sites could be included in educational curricula. Students could visit these sites instead of looking at display cases in museums, and such outings should result in better appreciation of Iowa's heritage, particularly the ethnic mosaic of that heritage. Thus the endeavors I have in mind go beyond being tourist traps. It is the authority and administration invested in an ethnic commission that could ensure this would be the case.

I certainly would want to see some of the economic profits circulate back into the educational sphere. This state has much to do by way of introducing ethnicity into its educational program. We need curriculum development in ethnicity in the public schools and universities, and this need includes courses, texts, films and projects of all sorts. In the universities we must further develop ethnic studies, inclusive of many groups, by pooling interdisciplinary talent and resources, and I see the integration of letters, history, political science, anthropology, and sociology necessary to this effort. At the very least, we should expect that the instruction in ethnicity would benefit from the development of sites, where the legacy of Iowa's many peoples would be portrayed.

But would the efforts of an ethnic commission be reduced to tasteless peddling of heritage, ultimately spoiling that heritage? To those who would answer yes, I understand their sentiment; it is a common one. But let us carefully consider the question: Will Indian culture or any other ethnic culture be more authentic in the absence than in the presence of an ethnic commission?

Indian traditions have already drastically changed, and such corruption is a fact for us all. If such change is lamentable, I prefer to look to the fact that Indians have not benefited enough from these changes. Furthermore, Indian heritage will continue to evolve, ethnic commission or not. The question is: To what degree will Indians control these changes and prosper from them? As I imagine it, the cultivation of Indian heritage by Indians, yes, even the marketing of their heritage with the help of an ethnic commission would increase Indian control over their own traditions, and the endeavor could bring meaningful employment to the state's Indian groups.

North American Indian tribes are currently bifurcated: these tribes are bisocial and bicultural, split into traditionalists and those oriented toward the larger society.[2] This division follows from tribal members being forced to decide whether to maintain Indian tradition and remain poor or to acculturate into White society with the hope of material gain. Currently, heritage preservation and economic development are often considered mutually exclusive. But this is not necessarily so, for with the support of an ethnic commission, Indians could combine economic development and increase control over their own heritage in a single effort. Specifically, Indians could simultaneously enhance their heritage and develop tourism and educational service in the form of restored heritage. Crucial to restoration efforts, the traditionalists would become economic resource people, in addition to heritage authorities, and their political leverage in decisions concerning heritage preservation should proportionally increase.

The political competency of the entire Indian community should increase in the course of their involvement in an ethnic commission. Experience gained in the politicized arena of an ethnic commission should result in Indians becoming better integrated into the total political process in Iowa. By making political alliances in an ethnic commission and otherwise expanding and sharpening their political skills, Indians would enhance their capacity to mobilize and focus their resources in the larger political arena. In this way, economic and political development of the Mesquakie settlement, for instance, actually would augment the ability of the Sauk and Fox to conserve their heritage.

Furthermore, if there would be economic development on the Mesquakie settlement, a decrease should occur in the emigration of youth, who must go elsewhere in search of employment. Employment would be brought to the settlement, providing jobs for the young. Generational continuity on the land would thereby be better maintained, a continuity several Indian panelists thought crucial to the preservation of Indian traditions.

However, economic development would also threaten Indian heritage. In the course of marketing it, even if only for instructional use, this heritage could become no more than a product, and those who transmit it could become no more than salespersons. Participation in the political process might have a similar effect. Indian heritage could be forever distorted by the pressures of the marketplace.

There is a formula by which those pressures can be brought under reasonable control, however. It is a formula that has its origins in Jewish shtetls of Europe.[3] Freed writes that in the shtetls there were two classes of people who played important roles in the preservation of Jewish traditions, the commercial and rabbinical classes. These two classes are roughly equivalent to White-oriented Indians and traditionalists.

Jewish traditions were conserved over centuries, and a partnership between entrepreneurs and rabbis accounts in significant ways for the preservation of this heritage. Businessmen — indeed all in the shtetl who had to find a living in the larger society — were understandably pulled away from Judaic traditions by the press of practical affairs. This would be the case with Indians as well. However, in the shtetl a special relationship between the rabbis and the people prevented the eclipse of Jewish traditions.

While Jewish merchants, tradespeople, workers, and peasants were busy at their tasks in the larger society, endeavors that inevitably brought pressures for assimilation, rabbis were through their studies preserving, or more precisely, elaborating on Judaic traditions, largely isolated from such pressures. As the rabbis commanded great respect in the community, their devotion to traditions and scholarship translated into the abatement of actual assimilation. This respect for rabbis among all the people was reinforced in the understanding among entrepreneurs specifically — men of influence who possibly had the greatest incentive for assimilation — that the rabbis were the ultimate authority on matters of heritage. However, given their relative isolation from practical affairs, rabbis were often unaware of minor infractions of traditional codes, granting entrepreneurs and others considerable latitude in their livelihoods. Thus the moral authority of rabbis was usually secure and seldom oppressive. The entire arrangement was solidified in the common practice of young rabbis marrying women from influential Jewish families. Economic practice and moral authority thus were made compatible in the shtetl and could be made so in the Indian community. The economic and political development of Indians through an ethnic commission could provide Indian traditionalists with the resources for the preservation and further elaboration of tradition, so long as moral authority, economic realities, and political practice are well matched in such efforts, as we know they can be.

NOTES

1. Oscar Handlin, *The Uprooted* (Boston: Little, Brown and Co., 1973), pp. 86–87.

2. See Malcolm McFee, *Modern Blackfeet: Montanans on a Reservation* (New York: Holt, Reinhart and Winston, 1972).

3. See S. A. Freed, "Suggested Type Societies in Acculturation Studies," *Minority Responses*, edited by Minako Kurokawa (New York: Random House, 1970), pp. 152–62.

13   Reflections of an Indian

DONALD GRAHAM

In this chapter Donald Graham reflects briefly on some of the factors, historical and contemporary, that have contributed to the high rate of alcoholism among American Indians. Mr. Graham is a Santee Sioux and therefore speaks from a high plains perspective, but his plea is ultimately for self-determination as a means for all Indians to maintain their identity and control their own future. He is concerned about the contemporary Indian, one for whom the past is important but for whom the past *is* past. That contemporary Indian is asking of America only what Chief Joseph asked a hundred years ago: that Indians be allowed to live as human beings, that they be recognized as such, and that they receive the same legal rights and protections as other people. It is an eloquent plea, one which can no longer go unheeded.

If the Great Spirit had desired me to be a white man, he would have made me so in the first place. He put in your heart certain wishes and plans. In my heart, he put other and different desires. Each man is good in his sight; it is not necessary for the eagles to be crows. Now we are poor but we are free. No white man controls our footsteps. If we must die, we die defending our rights.
— *Chief Sitting Bull, Hunkpapa Sioux*

Historically, American Indians were proud and resourceful people — able to cope with most situations arising in their daily lives. This great pride, coupled with unity of purpose — survival — created a way of life that was to be admired. The tribes had their own government, laws, justice, religion, and above all, unity. This unity enabled the Indian to provide for the needs of the immediate family and the welfare of the entire tribe. In the days prior to the coming of the reservation and the total dominance of the federal government, the Indian lived what seemed to the White society a carefree, almost childlike way of life. But the reality of Indian life included a very harsh existence governed by harsh laws, and in some eyes, a harsh justice. These were bred of grim living conditions. The climatic conditions of the open prairie were probably the most brutal of any place, save the steppes of Russia.

The total welfare of the tribe as an organization provided for the needs of individuals. If one was hungry, all were hungry. When the tribal hunters came back with food, everyone received a portion of it.

If a child was orphaned, the tribe or the relatives of the orphan took the child in; we did not have the problem of foster care. This brought about another sociological situation we wish we could see today: the extended family line, where the family was obliged to provide for the younger generation. By providing, I mean only for their immediate needs, for their welfare — not the handouts you see today.

The fierce pride, or way of life at that time, was something I could only term a beautiful existence — an existence that the Indian was condemned for by being on a collision course with the westward-moving White society. This collision course brought warfare not only between individuals but between armies and tribes. The warrior society was dedicated to maintaining the government, the laws, the justice of each tribe, and when it came time for combat, they were readily available and willing to die for their beliefs and their way of life.

Then came the most tragic period in American history, when a way of life and tradition were forcibly ended, when a self-sufficient people were put under military rule and pushed into a prisoner-of-war setting on the reservation. The reservations, fostered by the federal government and the United States Army, robbed the Indian of his pride, his will to compete, his will to provide for his own. They dictated sole dependency, or total dependency, on the government, promising that the government would see to all the needs of the Indian. Unfortunately, because the situation was born by force and greed, it did not quite work that way. The Indian was not a farmer in the first place. He was a nomad — a hunter. Trying to make the Indian a farmer brought about the total dependency I mentioned previously. There, I think, was the beginning of the problems built up over the last one hundred years and those we see today. I do not want to put all the blame on the United States government for what we now see. This total dependency is the largest contributing factor in the Indian's turn to antisocial behavior, primarily alcohol, as an escape mechanism. Alcoholism, the number one health problem of the nation, has affected the American Indian in epidemic proportions.

It would be easy to point fingers, to put the blame, but that is not my intent. This chapter was to touch briefly on what I felt about the past; and my feelings in this area are: The past *is* the past. The contemporary Indian, whose needs are not being met now, is the one I am concerned about.

When I see young Indian kids in a judicial system for antisocial behavior, such as drugs, alcohol, or willful mischief, this saddens me. Over the past few years, young Indian people have been taking on leadership roles for their people — whether they were trained for it or thrust into it. They ask for justice; they ask for social and economic change from within the system. This course of action, using existing laws to benefit all Indian people, and not adding to the burden of a country already torn by political, social, and economic strife, is the most logical. I am sure that militancy had its place, as well demonstrated in bringing the Indian situation to the national attention, and perhaps has its place today.

> We only ask for an even chance to live as other men live. We ask to be recognized as men. We ask that the same law shall work alike on all men.

It is quite difficult to think that these words were spoken by Chief Joseph of the Nez Perce Tribe in 1879. It is the very thing that we are trying to promote now. The point of unity that comes up quite often in this chapter is probably the most important issue to arise out of the new order of Indians. The seed of unity has lain dormant for over one hundred years. The seed is beginning to sprout and show results in that Indians are providing a united front in combating the numerous problems facing Indians nationwide.

The new order of Indians is asking that we, as Indians, be given the same chance to control our destiny as the rest of society. It is very important to maintain our identity as Indians, with special emphasis placed on our culture and tradition in all our activities. We do not wish to assimilate — only to be given self-determination for our future.

14 Give Me Back My People's Bones

Repatriation and Reburial of American Indian Skeletal Remains in Iowa

MARIA D. PEARSON

In 1971, Maria Pearson began the project for which she is perhaps best known regionally, nationally, and internationally: the reburial of Native American skeletal remains from public and private collections. Personally and spiritually outraged by the discriminatory handling of Indian versus non-Indian skeletal remains at an archaeological excavation near Glenwood, Iowa — the subject of this chapter — Pearson determinedly set out to transform long-established laws and professional procedures. Pearson's work in Iowa significantly anticipated the federal Native American Graves Protection and Repatriation Act (NAGPRA) of 1990. Since that time, Pearson has participated in many national and international conferences pertaining to reburial and repatriation issues of Native peoples.

I view archaeology as a science that is needed to help all people interpret their past and present. . . . This profession has the ability to impact our awareness of ourselves and our world . . . to assist in the realization of how our common humanity binds us to this planet. . . . Skeletal analysis has provided information on nutrition, disease occurrence and patterns, demography, warfare practices and migrations of Native people. I see the benefits of the study, being formally trained in archaeology, but I also comprehend another aspect of the universe that I give just as much credence and in fact more validity: the teaching of the belief in my ancestral tie to the earth and to a universal continuum that is more than what the study of skeletal remains can give to my existence. I make a choice every time I "discover" a burial. . . . I will not excavate a burial. I say this with the full knowledge of its ramifications to myself and to my discipline. However, I do so with the fullest amount of truth and integrity for my ancestors' existence and for my future generations.
—Benjamin K. Rhodd, Potowatami

I am Maria Pearson: *Hai-Mecha Eunka* or "Running Moccasins," a name my mother gave to me when I was a child. I am a member of the Yankton Sioux tribe in South Dakota. Now I live in Ames, Iowa.

Some thirty years ago, I had just married John Pearson, a civil engineer who worked for the Iowa Department of Transportation. He was their construction engineer in charge of building the interstate highway system in Iowa. When we got married, we moved out to southwest Iowa near Atlantic. We found a house in Marne and we bought it. I had six children from previous marriages, five boys and one girl, and they were little. We were attracted to this house because it had 200-year-old cottonwood trees. I remembered my grandmother who, five years before, had made her Spirit Journey. She always said, "Girl, remember that the cottonwood tree is sacred to the Sioux." And she told me the story of the circle of life and all that surrounded the cottonwood tree in our belief system. When I was a young girl, my grandmother did a lot of teaching to me of our own culture as we were drying corn, apples, or whatever was in season. She always said, "Girl, some day you are going to be called upon to stand up for what you believe in. You better know what you believe. Remember: don't ever let anybody make you angry, because then that makes you less than what you are. You'll always lose the battle when you are angry." All of these thoughts of my grandmother came to me when I looked at that house in Marne and saw all of those big beautiful cottonwood trees. I knew that is where I wanted to raise my children.

We purchased that house in 1969. I like to equate those times to the fact that I was starting a new life, Iowa had a new governor, and life was looking pretty promising. Only things turned out differently for me.

One day I was at home cooking dinner for my children and my husband. John came home from work and he said, "You know, honey, you are going to be upset when I tell you what happened at work today. Remember, about two weeks ago I told you that we located a cemetery in the right-of-way of an interstate highway near Glenwood and we were going to have to get the state archaeologist to check it out? Well, today that state archaeologist [Marshall McKusick] came in and located the graves for us in that historic cemetery in a place formerly called Pacific, Iowa, that no longer exists. Today that location is referred to as Pacific Junction. And they took out the remains of twenty-six white people, put them in new caskets, and took them to the local cemetery in Glenwood where they reburied them. They also found the skeletons of an Indian girl and her baby. They put those bones in a box and took them to the Office of the State Archaeologist in Iowa City for study."

Then I said, "John, that is discrimination! That goes against all of our beliefs."

John answered, "Well, I told you that you were going to be upset."

I finished making supper and put it on the table and said to John, "You'd better sit down and eat with the children. When you are done, you can see that they get their baths and go to bed." Then I went outside to the garden we put in when we purchased the house. I used to pray out there; I always felt closer to the Creator when I was outdoors. And that night, when I went out to pray, I heard the wind coming. I've always had a good relationship with the wind ever since I was a little girl. I heard the wind coming that night and it stopped just short of coming into our property. And in that pause, I knew that there was something different about to happen. Then a breeze continued into the cottonwood trees, and their leaves began to tinkle. The tinkling turned to a sound like crystal wind chimes, and there was a little crackling noise. That was the first time I had heard my grandmother's voice since she had made her Spirit Journey. She had always told me not to cry for her, because she would be in a far better place than I. But she also said, "If you ever need me, I will come to you in the wind. Listen for my voice." And that night, in Marne, in my garden, grandmother's voice said "Girl, I told you that you would have to stand up for what you believe in. You must protect the places where your ancestors lie."

And I said, "Grandma, I am scared! I live in this 'redneck' country; I have babies — they'll hurt my children!"

She answered, "No, your grandfathers are here. They will protect you. You must do this."

I said, "Grandma, I would not know what to do."

Grandma's voice said, "You are going to start with the very first thing. You will approach the white men from their place of understanding. You will go from there."

I protested, "Grandma, I don't know any of our medicine people. You always told me not to go near the graves of our ancestors."

Grandma responded, "Well, this is that time when you will need to take all of your strength and all of your courage to do this. But remember, you are not going to be walking alone. You will be walking with your grandfathers. Many things are going to happen to you, girl, as a result of this, but you are going to have to be strong, knowing that things will work out for you." And so, after a lot more conversation of things that were told to me that I cannot reveal, I went back into the house. My husband and children were already in bed, and my house was in order. When I went to bed that night, John asked me, "Honey, what are you going to do?"

I answered, "John, it is best that you do not know what I am going to do."

And I went to sleep.

The next morning when I got my husband off to work and the children off to school, I went into my closet and got out my grandma's trunk. I took out my moccasins and all of my cultural regalia and put them on. I put my hair in braids and fastened them with hair ties. Then I made that ninety-mile trip into Des Moines to the governor's office. And when I walked in, I was aware that people were looking at me, because in 1971 Indian women did not just walk around dressed in their regalia. When I came to the door of the governor's office, the receptionist [Kay Sterns] looked up and was startled to see me in my attire. I went up to her desk and she asked, "Can I help you?"

And I said, "Yes. I have come to see the Great White Father. You tell him that Running Moccasins is here."

She jumped up and she went back into the governor's [Governor Robert D. Ray] office. In a little while, she returned with this guy [Wythe Willey, Governor Ray's assistant] in a suit and a little black bow tie. He said, "Can I help you?"

And I asked, "Are *you* the Great White Father?" He said, "No," and I said, "Well, then you can't help me." He replied, "Well, the governor is a very busy man."

I answered, "Well, I am a very busy woman."

He asked, "What is it that you want to discuss?" And I replied, "You are not the Great White Father! I need to see *him*. You know, if I were an ambassador from a foreign country, you would have that red carpet rolled out all the way down Grand Avenue and out Fleur Drive to the airport. And you would have a delegation there to greet me! Well, I *am* an ambassador. I'm an ambassador for my people. And if this man, the governor, is over everybody in the State of Iowa, then he is over me and I have a right to see him."

The assistant turned around and he went into a back office. Then I looked up and there was the governor peeking at me around the corner of the door. I thought to myself, "He can't be too bad, because that is probably what I would be doing — peeking around the door to see who was there." The assistant returned and said, "The Governor will see you."

I went into the governor's office and in a glance saw these big over-stuffed black chairs with high backs. The governor was standing in front of his desk. He extended his hand to me and he said, "Have a seat, Running Moccasins."

I answered, "No, thank you. I can stand for what I have to say to you."

The governor asked, "Well, how can I help you?"

I said, "You can give me back my people's bones and you can quit digging them up."

The governor looked at his aide and asked, "Do *we* have her people's bones?"

And the aide said, "I don't know, but I'll find out!" A short time later, the assistant returned and said the matter had something to do with the Iowa Department of Transportation and the Office of the State Archaeologist. So I asked the governor, "Who is higher: you or that state archaeologist?"

The governor replied, "I am."

And then I asked, "Why doesn't the state archaeologist have to answer to you and the rest of us for what he does? If our taxes pay his salary, then I think he has some responsibility to report to us, you know. He won't return my phone calls."

The governor quickly replied, "Well, he will return *mine!*" He then picked up the telephone and talked to somebody. I could hear him say, "*Now* . . . in my office!" and he hung up the phone. I surmised that the governor had called the state archaeologist.

So I waited about five minutes. We were talking, and Governor Ray asked me, "How long has this been going on?"

I answered, "Well, let me see. How long have you been here? Five hundred years. For five hundred years you have been digging up our people." Knowing that the governor's mother was not well at that time, I asked him a question: "If your mother died and you buried her, what would you think if I decided to re-do my home in 'early white man' decor, and went to the cemetery and dug your mother up? What if I took her wedding ring? Or her glasses? I might want those glasses she wears. How would you feel?"

He gasped, "That's a *horrible* thought! That should not happen to anybody!"

"It happens to us and our people," I said. "Our children and grand-children are taking the impact of this emotionally and mentally. This has been happening to our people for five hundred years. And it is time for this to stop."

The governor asked, "Running Moccasins, how do you see this working?"

I said, "It works fine if you leave the dead alone. The dead are not without power, don't ever think they are. The dead have rights — the same rights as anyone of us here that make a decision as to where we want to be buried. We make those arrangements. The Indians that lived here a thousand years ago, or two thousand years ago, they did the very same things that we do today. They made those decisions of where they wanted to be — where they wanted to spend their Spirit Journey. And you interrupt that. That interrupts life for us here also. There are repercussions for all of this. I know one thing, governor, Indians are not the ones who created this problem. The white man created this problem, so the white man should accept the responsibility for rectifying this problem at no cost to the Indian nations." The governor agreed with me and wanted me to talk to the Iowa legislators about this problem.

In the meantime, I grew silent. The governor asked, "What is the matter, Running Moccasins?"

I answered, "Oh, I was just wondering."

"Wondering what?" the governor inquired.

I replied, "Wondering who is really boss."

The governor said, "I am! Why do you ask?"

I continued, "Well, I just know that if my chief had called me and I did not respond quickly, I know what would happen to me."

Then the governor grabbed the telephone again and had a brief conversation that ended with the words ".... did you ever hear about travel by airplane?" He then turned to me and said, "Well, Running Moccasins, I *will* pursue this and I promise you that I will look at this honestly."

I replied, "Well, governor, it's like this. You can either be a leader or you can be a follower."

He asked me, "What do you mean?"

I replied, "I guarantee you that this issue will be number one in five to ten years. And the choice is yours."

Agreeing with me, Governor Ray responded, "I would rather be a leader."

I said, "Then it is time to pick up that club and lead." And so, that is where the accepted practice of digging up American Indian skeletons in Iowa stopped and the plans to legally require the reburial of those remains already excavated in this state began.

The governor said, "I want to keep in touch with you and I want a telephone number where I can reach you."

"Well," I replied, "I'm scheduled for surgery tomorrow at Lutheran Hospital and I won't be at home, so you'll have to reach me at the hospital."

And so he said, "OK, we'll be in touch."

Then I went back home and told my husband what had happened up to that point. John replied, "Well, you can bet that life has just begun to rock your boat!" I guess he was right because I had heard the phrase, "You've got to paddle your own canoe." Right then I felt like I was the only one *in* that canoe and I knew I had some pretty turbulent waters to go through. And I was correct; that was only the very beginning.

In looking back, I think about what motivated me the strongest: I knew it was wrong to violate the dead and I also knew it was wrong to interrupt our ancestors' Spirit Journeys. But even worse, on the side of the living, was the violence that was erupting between American Indians and archaeologists. The Indian people had just come to the point where we could no longer tolerate the desecration of our ancestors. Newspapers had articles about the attempts by Indians to protect native cemeteries and photographs of people beating our Indian men in Michigan and Minnesota; and we had a stabbing in Sioux City at an ancient burial ground. To make matters worse, regarding my protest in what became known as "the Glenwood controversy," the State Archaeologist was quoted in the newspapers as saying, "I don't want that woman to think in any way that if she raises a fuss, I'll give her a couple of boxes of bones." I could not see the need for such anger and violence. I knew there must be a peaceful way to resolve this problem.

The next day when I was in the hospital, my doctor came in and said they were coming with a gurney to take me into surgery. He said, "You must be some kind of celebrity, Maria. You've got newspaper reporters out here wanting an interview and pictures of you. I don't know what is going on. I just know you are my patient and I've got to get you into surgery."

I happened to notice a reporter near the door and, in a loud voice, I said to my doctor, "I want to see my lawyer!"

The doctor gasped, "You are going into surgery, Maria. What do you need a lawyer for?"

I responded, "Well, you could kill me in surgery. I could die. And I want to will my bones to the State of Iowa: that way the state archaeologist won't have to dig me up and in so doing cause mental trauma to my children and grandchildren. You can give my bones to the state archaeologist since he likes Indian bones so well!"

On the following day, the Des Moines newspapers carried the news that "Running Moccasins wills her bones to the State of Iowa." That is when all hell broke loose around the state. The governor's office was bombarded with letters from the public that thought it was atrocious that state officials were grave robbing and creating havoc among Indians and other people. The governor let me read a lot of that mail, and there was a consensus that it was wrong to disturb the dead. Ultimately, the newspapers reported, "State Archaeologist asks Running Moccasins where she wants the Indian girl from Glenwood reburied." That was a real turnaround: a recognition of basic human values regarding the remains of the dead.

Next started a different phase of this controversial situation. I came through the surgery and I was at home recuperating. The community of scientists, archaeologists, and physical anthropologists asked me to come and tell them why we held our graves sacred. I remember one meeting that took place in Ames at the request of the professional archaeologists in Iowa. I called Don Wanatee at the Meskwaki Settlement and asked him if he would go with me. Don agreed, and met my husband and me at the that meeting. The woman in charge of introducing us said to the group, "Well, you have been wanting to hear from the Indians why they hold their graves sacred. Well, here they are. I don't care which one goes first." And that was our introduction!

I looked at Don and said, "This Dakota woman bows to the Meskwaki gentleman." So Don began by summarizing Meskwaki cultural history and traditional values.

It was very fascinating listening to him because Don is a great presenter of Meskwaki culture. He said, "There was a time when we went to the woods, and we all knew why we went to the woods. There was a time when we beat the drums, and we all knew what the drums were saying. There was a time when we sang our songs, and we all knew what we were singing. But now, today, the white man invades our graves and. . . ."

At that point, the woman in charge of the meeting interrupted, saying, "I'm sick and tired of you Indians trying to ram your culture down my throat! I don't give a damn whether you dig up my grandmother and take her wedding ring or not."

The other archaeologists at the meeting gasped in shock, and utter silence filled the room. Don attempted to speak in response but his voice fell silent. He put his hand on my shoulder and said, "Maria, you're going to have to tell them for us."

Don walked out of the room and left me alone with all those archaeologists. My first instinct was to be angry. At that moment I knew that I was a true Dakota woman, because I could have jumped across that table and ripped that woman's heart out with my bare hands! But I just looked at her and I said, "You invited us here to this meeting and then you insult us in this manner? Well, I came here to tell you something and I'm going to say it. You say you don't give a damn whether or not we dig up your grandmother and take her wedding ring. Number one, *we* DO give a damn! Indians do not steal from the dead nor do we disturb the dead. Second, *your* culture does not lie in this land, it lies across that ocean. You go over *there* and practice your grave robbing if you want and I won't bother you. Otherwise I'll fight you until there is no damn breath left within me to see that this does not occur again in my land." And then I said, "Thank you for your invitation," and I left the room.

My husband looked at me and said, "Woman, I have never been so proud of you as I am right now." We left Ames and drove back home to Marne. I remember thinking at that time just how hard this fight was going to be, because people simply did not understand common decency about the desecration of our burials.

After that there were many meetings with other archaeologists. I went to the national anthropology meetings in Washington, D.C. They asked me to come out there and speak, so I did. Our position is not a complex thing to understand and justify. Scientists claim that the study of Indian skeletons results in the betterment of humanity. But all of this grave robbing did *not* help humanity. The results of all of these studies were never even made available to the public at large. The reports were written in a language that only anthropologists could understand. The information was not applied in a way that helped the average person in this country. So there was no justification for robbing the dead.

In the meantime in Iowa, the governor called me one day and asked me to come to Des Moines and talk to the state legislature. Senator John Murray and Representative Bill Hutchins were the two that were sponsoring a bill to change the burial code of Iowa in order to better protect American Indian graves. They asked me how I saw the problem. I said that I saw this as the responsibility of the State of Iowa to prohibit the desecration of our graves and to set aside land on the east side of the state and on the west side of the state to rebury all of our ancestors that had already been dug up. They asked me if I would be willing to go out in these areas and find appropriate places to establish these reburial cemeteries. I said I would agree to do so if these cemeteries would be closed to the public so that the reburied remains would not be excavated again by collectors looking for Indian relics. These two cemeteries were established and the new legislation specified how the Office of the State Archaeologist was to proceed with the reburial of American Indian remains.

The skeleton of the Indian girl that was dug up at Pacific Junction was initially reburied in the Glenwood cemetery. Later her remains were moved to the Indian reburial cemetery in western Iowa. Soon after that it occurred to me that I had made a mistake. So I had to go back to the governor and tell him of my error. He asked, "Running Moccasins, what do you mean?"

I answered, "Remember that I told you we needed two cemeteries for the reburial of Indian remains — one in the east and one in the west?"

He said, "Yes, and you have them." I continued, "Well, I forgot that we Indians always relate things to the *four* directions. So we need a reburial cemetery in the north and one in the south." The governor replied, "Well, let's go get them." So now we have four Indian reburial cemeteries in the State of Iowa: in the west, the north, the east, and the south.

A new State Archaeologist, Duane Anderson, was appointed. We established an Indian Advisory Council for the Office of the State Archaeologist. I am the chair of that Council and have been since its inception. We had several conferences here in Iowa where we brought American Indian spiritual leaders, archaeologists, physical anthropologists, and other scientists together under one roof to find solutions to these problems. Duane Anderson and I worked pretty well together. We had an agreement: Duane was in charge of keeping the archaeologists in line, and I was in charge of handling the American Indian issues. We continue to meet with the present state archaeologist, Bill Green, quarterly or as the need arises when Indian burials are accidentally discovered in construction projects or uncovered through natural processes such as erosion.

Since the beginning of "the Glenwood controversy," I have traveled thousands of miles and I have lectured many places giving American Indian perspectives on reburial and repatriation issues. Our efforts in Iowa contributed to the passage of the federal Native American Graves Protection and Repatriation Act in 1990. It sometimes overwhelms me when I think of all the impacts the excavations of those burials near Glenwood had throughout the country and around the world. I knew initially it would be a hard fight to get our viewpoint recognized, but I certainly did not know in 1971 how far-reaching our concerns would be, into all the corners of the earth.

Here in Iowa, we no longer have any of our ancestors on shelves in cardboard boxes collecting dust. They have all been reburied and are continuing their Spirit Journeys.

A Closing Circle

Musings on the Ioway Indians in Iowa

LANCE M. FOSTER

The following essay, drawing, and poem illustrate Lance Foster's eclectic skills and are instructive as to American Indian world views, historical perspectives, and contemporary identities. Continuing the issue discussed by Maria Pearson in the previous chapter, Foster's essay underlines the sanctity of the Ioway's ancient burials here both in relationship to the tribe's traditional values and the identity of contemporary Ioway people today.

No Indians of any other Tribe dare build his fire or make a moccasin track, between the Missouri and Mississippi Rivers from the mouth of the Missouri, as high north as the head branch of the Calumet, Upper Ioway, and Des Moines Rivers, without first having obtained the consent of the Ioway Nation of Indians. In fact this Country was all theirs, and has been for hundreds of years. And this fact is susceptible of the clearest proof, even at this late day. Search at the mouth of the Upper Ioway River (which has been the name of their Nation time out of mind); there see their dirt lodges, or houses, the mounds and remains of which are all plain to be seen, even at this day, and even more, the Country which they have just claim to, is spotted in various places with their ancient Towns and Villages, the existence of which no Nation can deny. And even now their Village on the Des Moines is held and occupied by the Sacs — which place the Ioways only left about twenty-five years ago, on search of Game on other parts of their land, but never intended to abandon their claim to the Same or the bones of their fathers, which are yet to be seen there — and the Country has never been taken from them by Conquest.
—Watchemonne ("the Orator"), Ioway

Bakhoje min ke. I am an Ioway. Our ancestral lands were these lands between the two great rivers, the Mississippi, which we called *Nyitanga*, "the Great River," and the Missouri, *Nyisoje*, "the Turbid River." Appropriately, these lands still bear a variant spelling of our name, Iowa.

Our tribal name is spelled in different ways, though most often either Iowa (legally) or Ioway (culturally), based upon how different visitors with their different accents pronounced our name. The federally-recognized entity in which I am enrolled is officially designated "The Iowa Tribe of Kansas and Nebraska."

However, we called ourselves *Bakhoje*, a name we got from related tribes long ago. It seems that during our travels in prehistoric times along the larger rivers, we were camped on a sandbar during the winter. The Ioway were traveling with our close sister tribes the Otoe and Missouria. Suddenly a great gust of wind blew a mixture of the ashes from our many campfires over our lodges and all over our heads, causing our heads to become gray with the mixture. As a joke, the Otoe-Missouria called us *Bakhoje*, translated "Gray Heads," "Ashy Heads," or sometimes "Gray Snow." We have another name, *Chikiwere*, "the People of This Place," which we once called ourselves.

Our language is called Chiwere. This is the name by which our sister tribe the Otoe call themselves, and it means, essentially, "the People of This Place." Our language is of the Siouan family, and, although our closest relationships were with the Otoe, the Missouria, and the Hochunk or Winnebago, we also had ancient ties with the Omaha, Ponca, and Dakota. We did not always get along, but we always saw them all as related peoples.

Our oldest traditions indicate that many of our clans, such as the Bear, split off from our relatives the Hochungara (Hochunk or Winnebago), whom we also called our fathers or grandfathers, and whom we left behind near *Makashuje*, Red Banks, on the shores of Lake Michigan in Wisconsin. We left with our sister tribes the Otoe and Missouria, who continued on to search for new lands.

This fissioning process appears to have begun very early, perhaps as early as A.D. 700, but was finalized by the 1500s. No one is sure. However, the Ioway continued to visit their relatives the Winnebago, or Hochunk, into historic times. We have always recognized each other as kin.

Each of our clans had different traditions about their origins, different histories, and different religious rites, and the consensus seems to be that individual clans were originally separate ethnic groups who united to become one people in some long-ago time called *madadanyida*. Originating in other language families, some words survive in our own Siouan language.

Our stories indicate the Bear clan, and perhaps other clans such as the Thunder, went in search of new lands to escape the overcrowding and environmental and social stresses of the ancient homelands. Our ancestral travels seem to be marked by the effigy mounds they left in the shapes of bears, birds, and other shapes across the states of Wisconsin, Iowa, Illinois, and Minnesota.

The ancestral culture of the Ioway, Otoe-Missouria, and Hochunk, hallmarked by a distinctive type of pottery, left many sites across these midwestern states. Archaeologists have called this ancestral culture "Oneota," after a name for the Upper Iowa River where the culture was first discovered in the early part of this century.

From the east, we crossed *Nyitanga*, the Great River, the Mississippi. Here we thought we had found a new land, but when we landed on the shore, we found in the mud the footprints of others. In Iowa, we met other clans such as the Beaver. After a period of friction and warfare, our ancestral clans decided to make peace and unite as one people, the Ioway.

When the first French explorers entered the Land Between Two Rivers, they learned that these were Ioway lands. It is said that at one time, the Ioway had such power that a person of another tribe could not make a footprint anywhere in our territory without the Ioway knowing about it immediately, and that none could be here without our permission.

This was not because the Ioway were a particularly large tribe, but because we had been, according to our traditions, the first keepers of the Pipestone Quarries in southwest Minnesota, and because we had established a sacred covenant with the many natural forces and spirits who were the First Beings of the Land Between Two Rivers. These forces and spirits were our relatives, and would let us know about anything that was going on in our lands as soon as it happened.

For hundreds of years we moved along the rivers and streams of Iowa, building bark lodge villages, planting corn, beans, and squash, and hunting deer and buffalo in the woodlands and across the prairies. Our villages moved as garden soils and wood supplies became depleted, or sometimes due to frictions or whim. We moved freely across the lands that would become Iowa, as a man moves freely between the rooms of his house. In 1837, Grandfather No Heart defended our ancestral rights to these lands by producing a hand-drawn map showing our many villages and routes of travel.

Nothing lasts forever, and even before the French came, our lands suffered conflicts originating in events far to the east, primarily the Beaver Wars and the epidemics of disease that began decimating our people as early as the 1500s. Refugee tribes such as the Meskwaki, pushed west by events to the east in those bloody times, were generally welcomed and given sanctuary. Other tribes intruded aggressively, such as the tribes of the Illinois Confederacy, and they were expelled.

Those times remain bitter even in our memories today, with the game disappearing, incessant disease and warfare, and the intrigues of the European powers manipulating tribal alliances and enmities for their own purposes. At times, we experienced difficulties with our relatives the Sioux, the Yankton and Dakota, as well as the Osage and Omaha. We made new alliances with the Sauk and Meskwaki (erroneously known as the Fox) which sometimes went awry. Those were hard times, which it is better to try and put aside, for our tribes long ago made peace.

Ultimately, we were coerced into signing a series of treaties which forced us to retreat from our remaining lands in southern and western Iowa and northern Missouri. In 1836 we were pushed across the other great river, *Nyisoje*, the Missouri, and were established on a new reserve on the Nemaha River along the Missouri and the borders of what would become the states of Kansas and Nebraska. Here we were faced with our darkest times, for while there had been troubles and warfare in our Iowa homelands, we had at least had our freedom, and now we were prisoners on a small reservation that continued to be made smaller by more treaties, land speculators, and corrupt Indian agents. Social unrest was at its highest with the mounting pressures brought about by a surrounding white population that increased with every year, and by marriages outside the tribe that diluted our blood and traditions to the breaking point.

Finally, in the 1870s and 1880s, the last of the traditionalists said "Enough!" and moved south to Indian Territory (which would become the state of Oklahoma). Here we joined our old allies the Sac and Fox, and were near our relatives the Otoe-Missouria. Here we could live in the old village community, unlike the Iowa of Kansas and Nebraska who were pressured into breaking up communal lands into individual allotments. However, this situation in Indian Territory only lasted about ten years, before the white man once more forced the tribe to break up and accept allotment there as well. The white man's hunger for land was a force that could not be stopped, like the clouds of grasshoppers that devoured every plant in sight.

Now split into two federally-recognized groups, the Iowa of Kansas and Nebraska, and the Iowa of Oklahoma, we have learned to adapt to the changed conditions in the twentieth century. We hold jobs, scattered across the country, and often barely know our own relatives. The accounts of racism, fraud, and the loss of many of our ancient ways are well-known, an experience shared by every other tribe. This is a sad and long story of erosion of a people that once were the masters of the Land Between Two Rivers: a people barely remembered in that land which even yet carries their name, Iowa.

Now here we are, in the evening of the twentieth century. It is June, 1999, as I write this. The morning of the new millennium will soon dawn. But something has begun to happen in the last twenty years. The Spirits of our Old People, the *S'ageh*, have begun to call their lost children home, home to Iowa, the land that bears our name. According to what I understand, the process began in earnest with the dedication of the Ioway bark houses down at Living History Farms near Des Moines in 1982. At the dedication, Ioway from Oklahoma, including Solomon Kent, Nelson White, and members of the Big Soldier family, came up from Oklahoma and dedicated the site with ancient *Bakhoje* prayers.

A few days ago, I returned from a celebration held at Effigy Mounds National Monument in northeast Iowa. At the speakers' table, members of the Ioway, Otoe-Missouria, and Hochunk once more gathered as one people, something that had not happened at this locality for at least 170 years. It was in 1830 that our ancestors gathered across the *Nyitanga* at Prairie du Chien, to sign one of the treaties that would be used to remove us from these lands where our grandfathers and grandmothers sleep in the graves in the bluffs high above, where the mounds shaped like our Bear and Thunder ancestors cluster and march.

Having grown up in Montana, I came to Iowa State University in 1991, ostensibly to get my graduate degree in Anthropology (I would eventually add a graduate degree in Landscape Architecture as well). I would not have succeeded were it not for the many people there who helped me along the way, especially my major professor David Gradwohl, one of the editors of this collection. I accomplished some fruitful work, including my Anthropology thesis, "Sacred Bundles of the Ioway Indians" (1994) and my creative component for Landscape Architecture, "*Mayan Jegi* (This Land Here): The Ioway Indians and the Lost Landscape of Iowa" (1997). However, my real reason for returning to Iowa was to spend time in my ancestral home, visiting the sites of our *S'ageh*, understanding the seasons and elements, and connecting Ioway names of plants and animals to the actual plants and animals. For example, I had heard a story in which Trickster dresses as a woman, and uses the small seed balls of the sycamore tree as "tinkler" decorations. I finally held one of these balls in my hand, standing by *Nagredhe*, the Spotted Tree, the Sycamore, and thought of Trickster.

So many things have come to pass in my time in Iowa, the six years from 1991–1997. More and more Ioway and Otoe-Missouria have come to see this land their Old Folks told them stories about. The beauty of this place — the richness of the soil and its plant life — never fails to elicit wonder and joy. As I let my thoughts drift, I think of many such occasions.

Robert Fields, a Pawnee-Ioway-Otoe relative from Oklahoma with a Ph.D. in Anthropology, who taught for a time at Iowa State, brought his mother Esther Fields, Ioway-Otoe, to see the rich soil before she passed on.

In 1996, a conference on the Oneota ancestral culture, sponsored by the Office of the State Archeologist in Iowa City, brought members of the Ioway, Hochunk, and Otoe-Missouria together with archaeologists and other Oneota scholars. The high point for tribal members was the visit to ancestral sites in northwest Iowa, especially along Bear Creek, the Upper Iowa River, and finally at Effigy Mounds.

After a period of turmoil in the 1970s, our Yankton sister Maria Pearson led an effort that was joined by archaeologists in Iowa and resulted in new laws that protect burials and provide for reburial of the Old People. These Iowa laws, the first such legislation, became the model for other states, and ultimately provided the basis for the national law known as NAGPRA, the Native American Graves Protection and Repatriation Act. Our Ioway people support these efforts and hope that our Old Ones will be returned to rest as quickly as possible.

For me, much of the most enjoyable time has been spent with my relative Pete Fee. He is the son of my grandmother's sister, and in the Ioway tradition, this makes him my *Hinkayinye*, "Little Father."

Years ago, Pete lived in northeast Iowa, near New Albin, where he met his wife Alana. He returned with her to Kansas, where they spent the next twenty years raising a family. In 1998, Alana moved back to New Albin to be near family and Pete followed. Pete and his family now live there, with horses, on land near the edge of town. In Pete's words, "The spirits of our ancestors are here. I can feel them all around me. I feel good when I come back."

Pete and I talk often, although now that I work for the National

Park Service in Santa Fe, New Mexico, we do not get to see each other face-to-face as much as we used to during my days at Iowa State University when I would drive the five hours to Kansas for the powwow, a tribal election, or just to be with people I knew and trusted, and who knew and trusted me.

We talk now about this process which seems to have brought so many Ioway back to Iowa these last twenty years. It all seems part of a larger "something" that we cannot see clearly just now. We have talked about re-establishing a presence here in Iowa, somewhere where there is a lot, an acre, a patch of woods or a spring. There we would once more make the sacred connection, re-establish the ancestral covenant.

We talk about this. We will see. The *S'ageh*, the Old People, our grandmothers and grandfathers sleeping out there on the bluffs, made that covenant. Even now, perhaps they are guiding their wayward grandchildren to fulfill it once more.

ONLY STORIES

LANCE FOSTER ©1996

The Ioway Indians lived in Iowa for ages untold. Ioway culture and history were passed on through stories. Stories might be of the long-ago time or of prophecies for the future; the stories told people how to live in this world and how to prepare for the next one.

In "Only Stories," it is winter, the traditional time of telling stories. At this time snakes, the protectors of stories, were asleep and would not hear the stories they were told to defend by *Wakanda*, God. Here two families are visiting in the warmth of their lodge, the *chakiruthan*. One man is telling a story of the past as well as a story of the future. The time of the past, the coming of the Ioway clan ancestors, becomes the story of the future, the coming of a strange group of bearded white men with machines. Finally, the end of time becomes the beginning of time. In this way, everything becomes a circle and things are made right again. This is the way things have been and will be. This is what the stories tell us. As hard as it may be to believe, can we be certain that they are . . . "Only Stories"?

LIVING STONE

I am living stone
I am breathing water
I am a shaper of wind
I am a fragment of sun

The ages form and dissolve
and form me once more,
I hear the groaning of earth;
the murmur and shifting
The silence beyond
The darkness beneath
The tricklings of life's breath
Light is all around me, Time is all around me

I breathe it
As a living stone.

Lance M. Foster, Ioway

The American Indian in Iowa

A Selected Bibliography

GRETCHEN M. BATAILLE

This bibliography brings together many of the resources that concern the Indian in Iowa. The articles and books listed are uneven in their historical accuracy and reflect the differing perspectives on the subjects discussed; however, the listing should prove useful to persons interested in pursuing any of the specific areas in more detail.

Today, as we assemble here let it be known that we are to keep on thinking as one and to remember again what the Creator has planned for us, the reason why we are able to be here at this ceremony.

This location was where they came together for the first time, your people and the Mesquakies, where we purchased the land from the governor on which is now our village in Tama County. This is the only thing I am asking from Him: to give us to understand each other as one, and also to pray that we may continue to remind ourselves what he has given us, life. The Creator are we dependent upon, and not each other as mortals.

But, now, as life goes on and as our friendship has long ago been established, we are beginning to go in the opposite direction from one another as people because we may have forgotten the teachings and knowledge left by our ancestors.

Our forefathers had called upon the Creator and their religion in order to permit us to live here in this part of the country, Iowa. And our part in this ceremony, my son and I, is to affirm the first meeting in this building between our people, and to remember the original Mesquakies who came here to buy the land we now occupy, and to pray to heaven and earth that the friendship between us be as one, for continuance and reaffirmation, to the Creator, to help us in this endeavor.

The understanding which comes about at this gathering of our people today is intended, so that we may have faith in each and every one of us. So be it. That is all.
—This is the English translation of a benediction delivered in the Mesquakie language at the Old Capitol rededication ceremony in Iowa City, July 3, 1976, by Frank Wanatee, Sr.

While researching material for this bibliography on the American Indian in Iowa, I found an article about the 1918 Mesquakie Pow Wow.[1] I was not really surprised that the writer was condescending toward the Indians, nor was it unusual that he nearly fainted when Chief Young Bear spoke to him in English. After all, I reasoned, that was fifty-nine years ago. But then it occurred to me that in fifty-nine years there has been very change from that stereotype of the Indian.

Recently I asked a class of college students to write down all they knew about the Indian in Iowa. It did not take them long to jot down such items as "the Cherokee once lived here" and "there's a reservation north of Ames." Such reactions are not unusual in Iowa or elsewhere. The answers are a result of years of either ignoring the past or stereotyping the present. Many of these students who are otherwise well informed are sadly ignorant about the people of their own state. When they do discover that Indians live in Iowa, they mistakenly refer to the "reservation" at Tama, the "Iowa" Indians, or the "Tama" Indians—all incorrect labels for the 600 Mesquakie who live on a settlement near Tama, Iowa, where the land is owned by members of the tribe. Their misconceptions also reveal that if they know about the Mesquakie they do not know about the Indian populations of Sioux City, Cedar Rapids, or Des Moines. Knowledge about the Indian in Iowa seems to be stored away somewhere with romantic legends of Pocohantas from elementary school textbooks or thrilling childhood tales of battles and massacres.

Indians are not the "tourist attraction" in Iowa that they are in South Dakota or New Mexico, nor do they wield much political power. In fact, many people may have heard about the Mesquakie for the first time when tribal members went to court over their right to have voting machines on the settlement in the 1974 third district congressional elections or about the Indians in Sioux City when the memorial to Chief War Eagle was consecrated. This relative invisibility has both advantages and disadvantages. It is unfortunate, however, to lack political power in a time when Blacks, women, and children are being increasingly successful in equal rights movements. Nationally the American Indians have become visible through the Trail of Broken Treaties and Wounded Knee. In Iowa there have been isolated incidents that serve to make the population aware of the Indians: the interest of some church groups in aiding Indian causes, the inclusion of authentic Indian dancers at the 1973 Iowa State Fair, the voting dispute in Tama County, and the Omaha occupation of farmland along the Missouri River. But these incidents seem minor to most people and do not make the headlines.

Although the writers of the chapters included in this book sometimes mentioned these political or economic concerns, the focus remained on various aspects of education. Statistically, the education of American Indians is far behind the education of other groups in society.[2] But behind the statistics and studies is another, more significant reality: "Indian children in the twelfth grade have the poorest self-concept of all minority groups tested."[3] Why? It seems possible that while we acknowledge our inadequacies in teaching Indian students, we do not recognize that we are failing to teach other non-Indian students *about* American Indians. And so our children go on to become teachers and television producers and parents who perpetuate myths and racist stereotypes that contribute to the poor self-image of even more Indian children.

Senator John Culver argued in 1974 for funds for the new elementary school for Sac and Fox children on the basis that "education is a vital means of sustaining the cultural heritage, language, customs and ways of life for Indian Americans."[4] Education seems to be the key to a new understanding and awareness for both Indian and non-Indian people; Indian people need to be able to realize the promises of self-determination and non-Indians need to be educated about Indians so that they do not unintentionally thwart goals of self-determination.

This collection of material about and by the Indians in Iowa is needed especially by educators to help them implement the requirements of the revised Code of Iowa. Instruction in the history and culture of various minorities who have previously been overlooked or neglected in traditional studies is now mandatory.[5] It is hoped that this anthology and bibliography will provide the reader with insights into the history of the Indian in Iowa and will facilitate the understanding of the various views held by Indians in Iowa today.

The chapters reflect divergent views and at times are openly contradictory. Scholars of Indian affairs usually avoid referring to Indian "problems" because the term has too often suggested that it is the Indian who has the "problems." But these chapters do reflect the problems of definition and communication that make it nearly impossible to present a volume in which all authors express uniform views. Indians respected by their own culture may not have the credentials that grant automatic respectability in an academic environment. And academics, as several chapters suggest, often do not understand Indian perspectives. There are different opinions among Indians and non-Indians as well as among Indians themselves about certain aspects of tribal histories. The educational and instructional systems valued by one culture may not be equally valued by all, although education itself is a common value to all cultures.

For four hundred years the non-Indian has been trying to impose alien values and systems on the Indian. The time is long overdue to look at the diverse views and reexamine our own attitudes and values. Unless confronted with direct information, we often overlook the minorities within our state. Also we tend to absorb much incorrect information and racist material presented through mass media and, unfortunately, through textbooks. These books, often published by well-meaning authors, have perpetuated the inaccuracies portrayed in earlier publications.

Much has been accomplished recently in Iowa. The Citizens' Aide office now employs a person whose specialty is Indian affairs, and the Department of Public Instruction has increased its staff by the addition of an Indian education consultant. But two new positions in state government do not in themselves mean automatic understanding of the various Indian perspectives on contemporary issues, nor do they guarantee that the multiethnic guidelines mandated by Iowa law will be implemented immediately by all schools.

It is hoped that this collection and bibliography will help inform educators, students, and concerned people about the Indian in Iowa— the historical and the contemporary Indian. Iowa is a land rich in ethnic variety, but often we remember the heritage of those early pioneer farmers and forget that there were people living in the area long before the Iowa Territory existed. The descendants of those pioneers are still around, but so are those of the Sauk, the Fox, the Winnebago, the Sioux, the Iowa. . . .

NOTES

1. "Iowa Indians—Heap Big Pow Wow," *The Iowa Magazine*, 2 (Feb. 1918): 3–6, 22.

2. "Look at statistics in terms of Indian education as they are represented by the Senate subcommittee in 1970. Dropout rates are twice the national average; the level of formal education is half the national average; achievement levels of Indians are far below those of their white counterparts."—Herschel Sahmaunt (National Indian Education Association) at Iowa State University, April 18, 1974. "About 70 percent of the American Indian children in Iowa do not complete their elementary and high school education."—Dr. Donald Cox (State Department of Public Instruction) in the *Des Moines Register*, Feb. 14, 1975, p. 1.

3. Herschel Sahmaunt, Iowa State University, April 18, 1974.

4. In a news release from Senator John Culver dated April 11, 1974.

Gretchen M. Bataille

5. The 1975 Code of Iowa (Chapter 257.25) now states that instruction be required in the "history of the United States and Iowa with attention given to the role in history played by all persons, and a positive effort shall be made to reflect the achievements of women, minorities, and any others who, in the past, may have been ignored or overlooked by reason of race, sex, religion, physical disability, or ethnic background."

HISTORICAL AND BIOGRAPHICAL ACCOUNTS

Aldrich, C. "The Acquisition of Iowa Lands from the Indians." *Annals of Iowa* 7 (Jan. 1906): 283–90.

Anderson, Duane. "Iowa Ethnohistory: A Review, Part I." *Annals of Iowa* 41 (Spring 1973): 1228–41. "Iowa Ethnohistory: A Review, Part II." *Annals of Iowa* 42 (Summer 1973): 41–59. (Excellent source of information.)

Armstrong, Perry A. *The Sauks and the Black Hawk War.* Springfield, Ill.: H. W. Rokker, 1887. (Emphasis is on area of Rock Island; "factual" material is tainted with cultural biases of the times.)

Aumann, Francis R. "Mahaska." *Palimpsest* 41 (May 1960): 268–76.

———. "Poweshiek." *Palimpsest* 8 (Sept. 1927): 297–305.

———. "Wapello." *Palimpsest* 9 (Jan. 1928): 1–7.

———. "The Watchful Fox." *Palimpsest* 39 (July 1958): 289–300. (Biographical sketch of Keokuk.)

Baker, Paul E. *A Study of the Presbyterian Mission among the Mesquakie Indians in Tama, Iowa.* New York: Board of National Missions, 1960.

Barnhart, Cornelia Mallet. "Osceola and Oskaloosa." *Palimpsest* 28 (Oct. 1947): 300–309.

Barrows, Willard. "In the Neutral Ground." *Palimpsest* 3 (Apr. 1922): 106–24.

Beall, Walter H. "The Tegarden Massacre." *Palimpsest* 24 (Mar. 1943): 82–92. (Fayette County.)

Berthrong, J. D. "John Beach and the Removal of the Sauk and Fox Indians from Iowa." *Iowa Journal of History* 54 (Oct. 1956): 313–34.

Bicknell, A. D. "The Tama County Indians." *Annals of Iowa* 4 (Oct. 1899): 196–208.

Black Hawk (Ma-ka-tai-me-she-kia-kiak). *Autobiography.* Antoine Le Clair, U.S. Interpreter. Edited by J. B. Patterson. St. Louis: Continental Printing Co., 1882. (Reprinted 1932, State Historical Society of Iowa.) (Dictated in 1833 because Black Hawk wanted his story told; includes account of the Black Hawk War and brief comments on the histories of several Iowa counties.)

Blair, Emma Helen. *Indian Tribes of the Upper Mississippi Valley and Region of the Great Lakes.* Cleveland, Ohio: Arthur H. Clark Co., 1912.

Briggs, John Ely. "The Council on the Iowa." *Palimpsest* 39 (July 1958): 301–14.

———. "Indian Affairs." *Palimpsest* 21 (Sept. 1940): 261–77. (Discusses period from 1800 to 1840s.)

———. "Indian Affairs in 1845." *Palimpsest* 26 (Aug. 1945): 225–38. (About the removal of the Potawatomi and Winnebago from Iowa.)

———. "The Indian Cession of 1842." *Palimpsest* 23 (Sept. 1942): 287–97. (Review of the treaty.)

———. "No Sale." *Palimpsest* 22 (July 1941): 193–212.

———. "When Iowa Was Young." *Palimpsest* 6 (Apr. 1925): 117–27.

Brown, Richard Frank. *A Social History of the Mesquakie Indians.* Unpublished M.S. thesis, Iowa State University, 1964.

Busby, Allie B. *Two Summers among the Musquakies.* Vinton, Iowa: Herald Book and Job Rooms, 1886.

Caldwell, Hon. J. R. *A History of Tama County, Iowa.* 2 vols. New York: Lewis Publishing Co., 1910.

Call, Ambrose A. "Indians Repelled in Kossuth." *Annals of Iowa* 31 (Oct. 1951): 81–90.

Chapman, Samuel D. *History of Tama County, Iowa.* Toledo, Iowa: Toledo Times Office, 1879. (Early county histories are often limited in their perspective and may be biased against the Indians.)

Christensen, Thomas Peter. *The Iowa Indians: A Brief History.* Iowa City: Athens Press, 1954. (A collection of materials from newspaper files and county histories; includes a list of tribal chiefs.)

Cole, Cyrenus. *I Am a Man: The Indian Black Hawk.* Iowa City: Athens Press, 1938. (Published for the 100th anniversary of the death of Black Hawk; biography of Black Hawk and brief account of the war.)

Doe, John. "The Musquakas of Tama County." *Annals of Iowa* 8 (1870): 363–66.

Drake, Benjamin. *The Great Indian Chief of the West: The Life and Adventures of Black Hawk.* 7th ed. Cincinnati: G. Conclin, 1849.

Eby, Cecil. *"That Disgraceful Affair," the Black Hawk War.* New York: W. W. Norton, 1973. (Annotated bibliography of the Black Hawk War.)

Edwards, James G. "Indian Affairs." *Palimpsest* 10 (May 1929): 161–73.

Ferris, I. M. "The Sauks and Foxes." *Collections of the Kansas State Historical Society* 11 (1910): 333–95.

Foreman, Grant. *The Last Trek of the Indians.* Chicago: University of Chicago Press, 1946.

Froncek, Thomas. "I Was Once a Great Warrior." *American Heritage* 24 (Dec. 1972): 16–21, 97–99. (Well-written account of the Black Hawk War.)

Fulton, Alexander R. *The Red Men of Iowa.* Des Moines: Mills and Co., 1882. (Prehistory of Iowa; uses Schoolcraft, Parkman, Peck, and Drake as well as the *Annals of Iowa* and histories of Iowa counties. Represents ethnocentric biases of the times.)

Gallaher, Ruth A. "Indian Agents in Iowa, I." *Iowa Journal of History and Politics* 14 (July 1916): 348–94. "Indian Agents in Iowa, II." 14 (Oct. 1916): 559–96.

———. "Rantchewaime." *Palimpsest* 41 (May 1960): 277–83.

———. "The Tama Indians." *Palimpsest* 48 (July 1967): 289–99. (Reprint of 1926 article.)

Galland, Isaac. "The Indian Tribes of the West." *Annals of Iowa* 7 (Oct. 1869): 347–66.

———. *Iowa Emigrant*. Chillicothe, Ohio: William C. Jones, 1840.

Goodwin, David. "'Indian Look Out,' Below Iowa City." *Palimpsest* 54 (Jan.–Feb. 1973): 16–30. (A review of the legend and history.)

Grahame, Pauline P. "The Promised Land." *Palimpsest* 10 (May 1929): 187–98.

Green, Charles R. *Early Days in Kansas in Keokuk's Time on the Kansas Reservation*. Olathe, Kans.: Charles R. Green, 1913.

Gue, Benjamin F. *History of Iowa*. New York: Century History Co., 1903. (Limited material on Indians.)

Gussou, Zachary. *Sac and Fox and Iowa Indians*. Vol. 1. New York: Garland Publishing, 1974.

Hagen, William T. *The Sac and Fox Indians*. Norman: University of Oklahoma Press, 1958. (Historical and political study of the Sac and Fox from 1804 to the 1950s.)

———. "The Sauk and Fox Treaty of 1804." *Missouri Historical Review* 51 (Oct. 1956): 1–7.

Harlan, Edgar R. "Mesquakie Indians and the Wheeler-Howard Bill." *Annals of Iowa* 20 (July 1936): 381–84.

Hewitt, J. N. B. "Sauk." In *Handbook of American Indians*. Bureau of American Ethnology, Bull. 30, volume 1, part 2, pp. 471–80. Washington, D.C.: U.S. Government Printing Office, 1910.

Hexom, Charles Phillip. *Indian History of Winneshiek County*. Decorah, Iowa: A. K. Bailey and Son, 1913. (Weak account of the Winnebago in Iowa.)

Hickerson, Harold. *Sioux Indians*. Vol. 1: *Mdevakanton Band of Sioux Indians*. New York: Garland Publishing, 1974.

Hollmann, Clide, and Mitchum, John. *Black Hawk's War of 1832*. Philadelphia: Auerbach, 1973.

Hunter, W. A. "Refugee Fox Settlements among the Senecas." *Ethnohistory* 3 (Winter 1956): 11–20.

Hyde, George E. *Indians of the High Plains from Prehistoric Times to the Coming of the Europeans*. Norman: University of Oklahoma Press, 1959.

———. *Indians of the Woodlands from Prehistoric Times to 1725*. Norman: University of Oklahoma Press, 1962.

"Indians of Iowa." *Palimpsest* 50 (Apr. 1969). (Reprint of Feb. 1957 issue.)

Jackson, Donald, ed., *Black Hawk: An Autobiography*. University of Illinois Press, 1955.

———. "Black Hawk—The Last Campaign." *Palimpsest* 43 (Feb. 1962): 80–94.

———. "Black Hawk—The Man and His Times." *Palimpsest* 43 (Feb. 1962): 65–79.

Jones, J. A. *Winnebago Ethnology*, bound with Smith, Alice, *Economic and Historical Background for the Winnebago Indian Claims, etc.* New York: Garland Publishing, 1974.

Kantor, MacKinlay. *Spirit Lake.* Cleveland: Cleveland World Publishing Co., 1961.

Kellogg, Louise. "The Fox Indians during the French Regime." *Wisconsin State Historical Society Proceedings* 55 (1907): 142–88.

Lee, L. P., ed. *History of the Spirit Lake Massacre.* New Britain, Conn.: L. P. Lee, 1857.

Lowie, R. H. *Indians of the Plains.* New York: McGraw–Hill Book Co., 1954.

Mahan, Bruce E. "The Great Council of 1825." *Palimpsest* 6 (Sept. 1925): 305–18.

———. "Making the Treaty of 1842." *Palimpsest* 10 (May 1929): 174–80.

———. "Moving the Winnebago." *Palimpsest* 3 (Feb. 1922): 33–52.

Marsh, C. *Expedition of the Sacs and Foxes.* Collections of Kansas State Historical Society 15 (1900): 104–55.

Michelson, Truman. *Autobiography of a Fox Woman.* 40th Annual Report of the Bureau of American Ethnology to the Secretary of the Smithsonian Institution, 1918–1919, pp. 291–349. Washington, D.C.: U.S. Government Printing Office, 1925.

Mitchell, Leland. "Crying in the Bottoms." *Palimpsest* 26 (Aug. 1945): 239–46. (Account of Sauk and Fox migration west of the Missouri River in 1845.)

Oswalt, Wendall H. *This Land Was Theirs: A Study of the North American Indian.* New York: John Wiley and Sons, 1966. (See pp. 216–61, "The Fox.")

Peake, Ora Brooks. *A History of the U.S. Indian Factory System, 1795–1822.* Denver: Sage Books, 1954.

Petersen, William. "Buffalo Hunting with Keokuk." *Palimpsest* 46 (May 1965): 257–72. (Much of Petersen's writing comes from secondary sources and should be approached with skepticism.)

———. "Governor Chambers' First Annual Message." *Palimpsest* 36 (Dec. 1955): 493–98. (Dec. 8, 1841.)

———. "Iowa in the Louisiana Purchase." *Palimpsest* 35 (Sept. 1954): 357–67.

———. "The Ioways Bid Farewell." *Palimpsest* 19 (Oct. 1938): 397–400.

———. "Jean Marie Cardinal." *Palimpsest* 12 (Nov. 1931): 414–20.

———. "The Joliet-Marquette Expedition." *Palimpsest* 49 (Oct. 1968): 416–46.

———. "Julien Dubuque." *Palimpsest* 47 (Mar. 1966): 105–19.

———. "Perrot's Mines." *Palimpsest* 12 (Nov. 1931): 405–13.

———. "The Second Purchase." *Palimpsest* 18 (Mar. 1937): 88–97.

———. "The Spirit Lake Massacre." *Palimpsest* 43 (Oct. 1962): 433–76.

———. *The Story of Iowa.* New York: Lewis Historical Publishing Co., 1952.

———. "Tama Indians in 1967." *Palimpsest* 48 (July 1967): 320.

———. "The Terms of Peace." *Palimpsest* 43 (Feb. 1962): 95–111. (Black Hawk War.)

———. ed. *Two Hundred Topics in Iowa History.* Iowa City: State Historical Society, 1932.

————. "The Winnebago Indians." *Palimpsest* 61 (July 1960): 325–56.

Peterson, Harold D. "Wahkonsa." *Palimpsest* 23 (Apr. 1942): 121–35. (Fictionalized biographical sketch of the son of Chief Umpashota.)

Plank, P. "The Iowa Sac and Fox Indian Mission." *Transactions of the Kansas State Historical Society* 10 (1908): 312–25.

Pruitt, O. J. "The Indian Battle Near Crescent." *Annals of Iowa* 32 (Jan. 1955): 541–43.

Purcell, L. Edward. "The Mesquakie Indian Settlement in 1905." *Palimpsest* 55 (Mar.–Apr. 1974): 34–55. (Excellent.)

Quimby, G. I. *Indian Life in the Upper Great Lakes.* Chicago: University of Chicago Press, 1960. (11,000 B.C. to A.D. 1800.)

Ramer L. V. *The Migrations of the Sauk and Fox Indians.* Unpublished M.A. thesis, State University of Iowa, 1936.

Rayman, Ronald A. "Joseph Montfort Street: Establishing the Sac and Fox Indian Agency in Iowa Territory, 1838–1840." *Annals of Iowa* 43 (Spring 1976): 261–74.

Rebok, Horace M. "The Last of the Mus-qua-kies." *Iowa Historical Record* 17 (July 1901): 305–35.

Richman, Irving Berdine. *Ioway to Iowa.* Iowa City, Iowa: State Historical Society of Iowa, 1931. (More emphasis on White settlement of Iowa than Indian territory, though key events are referred to; includes vignettes that might appeal to junior high level students.)

Ritzenthaler, Robert, and Ritzenthaler, Pat. *The Woodland Indians.* Garden City, N.Y.: Natural History Press, 1970.

Sabin, Henry. *The Making of Iowa.* Chicago: A. Flangan, 1900.

"Sac and Fox Indian Council of 1841." *Annals of Iowa* 12 (July 1920): 322–31. (Verbatim account of a meeting between representatives of the Sac and Fox and government officials.)

"Sac and Fox Indian Council of 1842." *Annals of Iowa* 12 (July 1920): 331–45.

Sage, Leland L. *A History of Iowa.* Ames: Iowa State University Press, 1974. (Very little on Indians.)

Schmidt, John F. *A Historical Profile of Sioux City.* Sioux City, Iowa: Sioux City Stationary Co., 1969.

Schwieder, Dorothy, ed. *Patterns and Perspectives in Iowa History.* Ames: Iowa State University Press, 1973. (Contains one article on the Sac and Fox.)

Sharp, Abbie Gardner. *History of the Spirit Lake Massacre and Captivity of Miss Abbie Gardner.* Des Moines: Homestead Printing Co., 1910.

Spencer, John W., and Burrows, J. W. D. *The Early Days of Rock Island and Davenport.* Chicago: Lakeside Press, 1942.

Stevens, Frank E. *The Black Hawk War Including a Review of Black Hawk's Life.* Chicago: F. E. Stevens, 1903. (Anti-Sauk bias.)

Stout, David B. *Sac and Fox and Iowa Indians.* Vol. 2: *Indians of East Missouri, West*

Illinois and South Wisconsin, from the Proto-Historic Period of 1804. New York: Garland Publishing, 1974.

Swisher, Jacob A. "Chief Waubonsie." *Palimpsest* 29 (Dec. 1948): 353–61. (Chief of the Potawatomi, 1812.)

———. "The Half-Breed Track." *Palimpsest* 14 (Feb. 1933): 69–76.

———. "War Eagle." *Palimpsest* 30 (Feb. 1949): 33–41. (Last Sioux chief to dwell in Iowa; monument dedicated in 1922.)

———. "With the Indians." *Palimpsest* 22 (Sept. 1941): 278–85. (View of Indian-White relations during the 1840s.)

Teakle, Thomas. *The Spirit Lake Massacre.* Iowa City: Iowa State Historical Society, 1918.

Temple, Wayne C. *Indian Villages of the Illinois Country: Historic Times.* Springfield: Illinois State Museum, 1958.

Thwaites, Reuben G. *The Story of the Black Hawk War.* Madison: State Historical Society, 1892.

U.S. Bureau of Indian Affairs. *Indians of the Central Plains.* Washington, D.C.: U.S. Government Printing Office, 1968.

Wakefield, John A. *Wakefield's History of the Black Hawk War.* Jacksonville, Ill.: Calvin Goudy, 1834. (Account of the 1832 Black Hawk War and the beginning of White settlement in Iowa.)

Ward, Duren J. H. "Meskwakia." *Iowa Journal of History and Politics* 4 (Apr. 1906): 179–89.

Washburn, Wilcomb. *The American Indian and the United States: A Documentary History.* 4 vols. New York: Random House, 1973.

EDUCATION AND THE INDIAN IN IOWA

Allinson, MacBurnie. *Education and the Mesquakie.* Unpublished Ph.D. dissertation, Iowa State University, 1974.

Almquist, Rex B. *Educational History of Iowa Sac and Fox, Present Problems in School and Community: Implications for Social Work.* Unpublished M.S. thesis, State University of Iowa, 1972.

Byrd, John M. *Educational Policies of the Federal Government toward the Sac and Fox Indians of Iowa, 1928–1937, with Resulting Changes in Indian Educational Attitudes: A Study in the Process of Assimilation.* Unpublished M.S. thesis, State University of Iowa, 1938.

Hoyt, Elizabeth E. "The Children of Tama." *Journal of American Indian Education* 3 (Oct. 1963): 15–20.

Jones, Ben. *Economic, Legal and Educational Status of the Mesquakie (Fox) Indian of Iowa.* Unpublished M.A. thesis, State University of Iowa, 1931.

Mather, P. Boyd. "Tama Indians Fight for Their Own Schools." *Christian Century* 85 (Oct. 2, 1968): 1251–52.

Ricchiardi, Sherry. "Alarming Drop-out Rate of Indian Youths Prompts New Programs." *Des Moines Register*, 16 Dec. 1973, p. 5E.

Swisher, Jacob A. "Iowa Schools in 1846." *Palimpsest* 27 (Mar. 1946): 65–74.

LANGUAGE, LINGUISTICS, LITERATURE, AND ART

(See Murdock's *Ethnographic Bibliography of North America* for a more complete listing of articles on language and linguistics.)

Aumann, Francis R. "Indian Oratory." *Palimpsest* 39 (July 1958): 315–20. (Black Hawk and Keokuk.)

Bloomfield, L. "Notes on the Fox Languages." *International Journal of American Linguistics* 3 (1925): 219–32; 4 (1927): 181–219.

Briggs, John Ely. "The Geneology of a Legend." *Palimpsest* 22 (Sept. 1941): 286–88. (Describes how stories become legends; specifically refers to Fulton's *The Red Men of Iowa*.)

Cleven, Catherine Seward. *Black Hawk, Young Sauk Warrior*. Indianapolis: Bobbs-Merrill, 1966. (Juvenile literature.)

Derleth, August W. *Wind over Wisconsin*. New York: Scribner's, 1938. (Fiction.)

Frederick, John T. "Black Hawk and White Men." *Palimpsest* 36 (Oct. 1955): 391–406. (Analysis of novels about Black Hawk.)

Fugle, Eugene. "Mesquakie Witchcraft Lore." *Plains Anthropologist* 6 (1961): 31–39.

Fuller, Iola. *The Shining Trail*. New York: Duell, Sloan, and Pearce, 1943. (Fiction.)

Hallet, Richard. *Michael Beam*. New York: Houghton, 1939. (Fiction.)

Harlan, Edgar R. "Some Methods of Collecting Indian Lore." *Annals of Iowa* 18 (Oct. 1932): 403–12.

Horan, James D., ed. *The McKenney-Hall Portrait Gallery of American Indians*. New York: Crown Publishing, 1972. (Includes excellent color portraits of Indians of Iowa.)

———. "Four Chiefs, One Brave, and Beautiful Flying Pigeon." *The Iowan* 25 (Dec. 1976): 23–32.

Huot, Martha C. "Two Fox Peyote Songs." *Transition* 24 (June 1936): 117–20.

Jones, William. "Algonquian." *Bull. of the Bureau of American Ethnology* 49 (1911): 735–873.

———. "Episodes in the Culture-Hero Myth of the Sauks and Foxes." *Journal of American Folklore* 14 (Oct.–Dec. 1901): 225–39.

———. *Fox Texts*. Publications of the American Ethnological Society. Vol. 1. Leyden, 1907.

Lasley, Marie. "Sac and Fox Tales." *Journal of American Folklore* 15 (July–Sept. 1902): 170–78. (Mrs. Lasley is the daughter of Black Hawk.)

Lay, Permilia Robinson. "Mesquakie Crafts Are Valued and Preserved." *Iowan* 22 (Winter 1973): 10–13.

McTaggart, Frederick E. *Mesquakie Stories: The Teachings of the Red Earth People.*

Unpublished Ph.D. dissertation, State University of Iowa, 1973. (A study of the oral tradition as it still exists.)

————. *Wolf That I Am; In Search of the Red Earth People.* Boston: Houghton Mifflin, 1976. (Narrative account of the author's visits to the Mesquakie Settlement to learn about the oral tradition.)

Mahan, Bruce E., and Gallaher, Ruth A. *Stories of Iowa for Boys and Girls.* New York: Macmillan, 1929. (Juvenile fiction.)

Meigs, Cornelia. *As the Crow Flies.* New York: Macmillan, 1937. (Fiction.)

Michelson, Truman. "Miss Owen's Folklore of the Musquakie Indians." *American Anthropologist,* n.s. 38 (Jan.–Mar. 1936): 143–45.

Moore, Francis Roy. *Wapello Chief: A Tale of Iowa.* Cedar Rapids: Torch Press, 1938. (Fiction.)

Owen, Mary Alicia. *Folk-Lore of the Musquakie Indians of North America.* London: David Nutt, 1904.

Petersen, William. "The Red Man in Real Life." *Palimpsest* 51 (Mar. 1970): 131–67. (Review of pictorial and fictional accounts of Indians.)

Pruitt, O. J. "Some Iowa Indian Tales." *Annals of Iowa* 32 (Jan. 1954): 203–16.

Skinner, Alanson. "Sauk Tales." *Journal of American Folklore* 41 (Jan.–Mar. 1928): 147–71.

Voorhis, Paul H. "New Notes on the Mesquakie (Fox) Language." *International Journal of American Linguistics* 37 (Apr. 1971): 63–75.

SOCIAL, POLITICAL, AND CULTURAL ORGANIZATION

(See Murdock's *Ethnographic Bibliography of North America* for additional articles.)

Brown, R. F. *A Social History of the Mesquakie Indians, 1800–1963.* Unpublished M.A. thesis, Iowa State University, 1964.

Burford, C. C. "Sauk and Fox Indian Ceremonials Attract Large Audiences and Wide-spread Interest." *Journal of the Illinois State Archaeology Society* 5 (1947): 24–30.

Callender, C. *The Social Organization of the Central Algonkians.* Milwaukee Public Museum Publications in Anthropology, Number 7. Milwaukee, Wis., 1962.

Coe, Lulu Mae. "Youngsters Thrilled by Real Live History, the Chief." *Des Moines Register,* 7 Oct. 1947, p. 3.

English, Emory H. "A Mesquakie Chief's Burial." *Annals of Iowa* (3rd series) 30 (Jan. 1951): 545–50.

Flannery, R. "Two Concepts of Power." *Proceedings of the International Congress of Americanists* 29 (1952): 185–89.

Forsyth, T. "Account of the Manners and Customs of the Sauk and Fox Nations." In *The Indian Tribes of the Upper Mississippi Valley.* Edited by E. H. Blair. Cleveland: Arthur H. Clark Co., 1911.

Fruhling, Larry. "Maverick Indian Is Bone in the Tribal Throat." *Des Moines Tribune,* 20 May 1976, pp. 1, 24.

Gearing, Frederick. *The Face of the Fox*. Chicago: Aldine Publishing Co., 1970. (Account of the University of Chicago Fox Project, 1952–57.)

———. "Today's Mesquakies." *The American Indian* 7 (1955): 24–37.

Gearing, Frederick; Netting, Robert M.; and Peattie, Lisa R. *Documentary History of the Fox Project: 1948–1959*. Chicago: Department of Anthropology, University of Chicago, 1960.

Green, O. J. "The Mesquakie Indians." *Red Man* 5 (1912): 47–52, 104–9.

Harrington, Mark. "Sacred Bundles of the Sac and Fox Indians." University of Pennsylvania, University Museum, *Anthropological Publications* 4 (1914): 125–262.

Hoyt, Elizabeth E. *Tama: An American Conflict*, Unpublished manuscript, Iowa State University, 1964.

"Iowa Indians— Heap Big Pow Wow." *The Iowa Magazine* 2 (Feb. 1918): 3–6, 22. (An account of the 1917 Mesquakie Pow Wow; the writer is condescending and ignorant of Indian culture.)

Joffe, Natalie F. "The Fox of Iowa." In *Acculturation in Seven American Indian Tribes*. Edited by Ralph Linton, pp. 259–331. New York: D. Appleton-Century, 1940. (Social and political organization and relations between Indians and Whites.)

Johnson, Steven. "Women Are More Active in Tama Indian Pow Wow." *Des Moines Register*, 11 Aug. 1972, p. 5.

Johnson, Willard L. *The Religion of the Mesquakie Indians in Tama County, Iowa*. Unpublished M.A. thesis, Drake University, 1932.

Jones, William. "The Algonkin Manitou." *Journal of American Folklore* 18 (July–Sept. 1905): 183–90.

———. *Ethnography of the Fox Indians*. Edited by Margaret Welpley Fisher. Bureau of American Ethnology, Bull. 125. Washington, D.C.: U.S. Government Printing Office, 1938. (General discussion of Mesquakie social organization and material culture.)

———. "The Heart of the Brave." *Harvard Monthly* 30 (1900): 99–106.

———. "Mortuary Observances and the Adoption Rites of the Algonquin Foxes of Iowa." *International Congress of Americanists* (15th Session) 1 (1907): 263–77.

Jones, William. "Notes on the Fox Indians." *Journal of American Folklore* 24 (Apr.–June 1911): 209–37.

Knauth, Otto. "A Rare Turn of the Century Look at Tama's Proud Mesquakie Indians." *Des Moines Register Picture Magazine*, 17 Feb. 1974, pp. 10–12.

Mamak, Alexander. "The Traditional Authority Systems of the Sac and Fox Indians." *Mankind* 10 (Jan.–Mar. 1970): 135–47.

Michelson, Truman. "The Changing Character of Fox Adoption Feasts." *American Journal of Sociology* 34 (Mar. 1929): 890–92.

———. "Contributions to Fox Ethnology." *Bureau of American Ethnology*, Bull. 85 (1927): 1–162; 95 (1930): 1–183. Washington, D.C.: U.S. Government Printing Office.

————. *Fox Miscellany*. Bureau of American Ethnology, Bull. 114. Washington, D.C.: U.S. Government Printing Office, 1937.

————. "How Meskwaki Children Should Be Brought Up." In *American Indian Life*. Edited by Dr. E. C. Parsons, pp. 81–86. New York: Viking Press, 1925.

————. *Notes on the Fox Wapanowiweni*. Bureau of American Ethnology, Bull. 105. Washington, D.C.: U.S. Government Printing Office, 1932.

————. "Notes on the Social Organization of Fox Indians." *American Anthropologist*, n.s. 15 (Oct.–Dec. 1913): 691–93.

————. *Observations on the Thunder Dance of the Bear Gens of the Fox Indians*. Bureau of American Ethnology, Bull. 89. Washington, D.C.: U.S. Government Printing Office, 1929.

————. *The Owl Sacred Pack of the Fox Indians*. Bureau of American Ethnology, Bull. 72. Washington, D.C.: U.S. Government Printing Office, 1921.

————. "Ritualistic Origin Myths of the Fox Indians." *Journal of the Washington Academy of Sciences* 6 (1916): 209–11.

————. *Sauk Notebook*. Bureau of American Ethnology, ms. 2736. Washington, D.C., 1913.

————. "Sol Tax on the Social Organization of the Fox Indians." *American Anthropologist*, n.s. 40 (Jan.–Mar. 1938): 177–79.

————. "Some General Notes on the Fox Indians." *Journal of the Washington Academy of Sciences* 9 (1919): 483–94, 521–28, 593–96.

————. "What Happened to Green Bear Who Was Blessed with a Sacred Pack." Bureau of American Ethnology, Bull. 119 (1938): 161–76.

Miller, W. B. "Two Concepts of Authority." *American Anthropologist*, n.s. 57 (Apr. 1955): 271–89.

Mooney, James, and Thomas, Cyrus. "Foxes." In *Handbook of American Indians*. Bureau of American Ethnology, Bull. 30, part 1, pp. 472–74. Washington, D.C.: U.S. Government Printing Office, 1907.

Neff, Ronald L., and Weinstein, Jay A., "Iowa's Indians Come of Age." *Society* 12 (1975): 22–26. (Discussion of recent political involvement of the Mesquakie.)

Nichols, Roger L. "A Missionary Journey to the Sac-Fox Indians, 1834." *Annals of Iowa* 36 (Spring 1962): 301–15.

Owen, R. C.; Deetz, J. J. F.; and Fisher, A. D. *The North American Indians: A Sourcebook*. New York: Macmillan, 1967.

Peattie, Lisa Redfield. *Being a Mesquakie Indian*. Chicago: Department of Anthropology, University of Chicago, 1950.

Polgar, Steven. "Biculturation of Mesquakie Teenage Boys." *American Anthropologist*, n.s. 62 (Apr. 1960): 217–35.

Randall, Helen. "Indian Life-Styles in Iowa's Urban Settings." *Des Moines Register*, 6 Aug. 1973, p. 13.

Ricchiardi, Sherry. "Cultural Pride of Iowa's Indians." *Des Moines Register*, 5 Aug. 1973, pp. 1E, 4E.

———. "Indians, Chicanos Organize Prison Cultural Center." *Des Moines Register*, 7 July 1974, p. 7E.

———. "Indian Thanksgiving: A Time of Sharing." *Des Moines Register*, 28 Nov. 1974, pp. 1, 3.

———. "The Voice of Youth behind the Indian Movement." *Des Moines Register*, 7 Aug. 1973, p. 9.

Skinner, Alanson. "Ethnology of the Iowa Indians." *Bull. of the Public Museum of the City of Milwaukee* 5 (1926): 181–354. (General summary of Ioway Indian material culture.)

———. "Observations of the Ethnology of the Sauk Indians." *Bull. of the Public Museum of the City of Milwaukee* 5 (1923–25): 1–180. (General summary of Sauk social organization and material culture.)

———. "Sauk War Bundles." *Wisconsin Archaeologist* 2 (1923): 148–50.

———. "Societies of the Iowa." *Anthropological Papers of the American Museum of Natural History* 11 (1915): 679–740. (Ioway Indian ritual organization.)

———. "Summer among the Sauk and Ioway Indians." *Yearbook, Public Museum of the City of Milwaukee* 2 (1922): 6–15.

———. "Traditions of the Iowa Indians." *Journal of American Folklore* 38 (Oct.–Dec. 1925): 425–506.

Smith, Huron H. "Ethnobotany of the Meskwaki Indians." *Bull. of the Public Museum of the City of Milwaukee* 4 (1928): 175–326. (Discussion of the use of plants in Mesquakie culture.)

———. "The Red Earth Indians." *Yearbook, Public Museum of the City of Milwaukee* 3 (1923): 27–38.

Spencer, Dick. "Powwow Time." *Palimpsest* 48 (July 1967): 300–319. (History of annual August powwows on the Mesquakie settlement.)

Stucki, Larry R. "Anthropologists and Indians: A New Look at the Fox Project." *Plains Anthropologist* 12 (1967): 300–317.

Tax, Sol. "The Fox Project." *Human Organization* 17 (Spring 1958): 17–19. (University of Chicago Project with the Mesquakie.)

———. "Integration and the Indian." *Wisconsin Magazine of History* 41 (Winter 1957–58): 99–101.

———. "The Social Organization of the Fox Indians." In *Social Anthropology of North American Indian Tribes*. 2nd ed. Edited by Fred Eggan, pp. 243–84. Chicago: The University of Chicago Press, 1955. (Detailed study of Mesquakie kinship patterns.)

Witten, Edward. "Indians Seek Community Control." *The New Leader* 53 (Feb. 2, 1970): 15–17.

Yeast, William E. "The Mesquakie Memorial Feast." *Annals of Iowa* 36 (Spring 1963): 591–98.

Zielinski, John M. *Indians*. Kalona, Iowa: Photo-Art Gallery, 1972. (Photographs.)

———. *Mesquakie and Proud of It*. Kalona, Iowa: Photo-Art Gallery, 1976. (Mostly

contemporary view of Mesquakie; illustrated by Zielinski's photographs and
drawings by Leonard Young Bear.)

———. "What Being an Indian is Like." *Des Moines Register Picture Magazine,* 27
Apr. 1975, pp. 4–7.

Zielinski, Mary. "The Beat of the Tribal Drums Still Echoes at Tama." *The Iowan*
20 (15 Mar. 1972): 10–16.

ARCHAEOLOGY AND PREHISTORY

(More literature on this subject may be found in the *Journal* of the Iowa
Archaeological Society and Reports of the Office of the State Archaeologist.)

Anderson, Duane. "The Development of Archeology in Iowa: An Overview."
Proceedings of the Iowa Academy of Science 82 (1975): 71–86.

———. *Western Iowa Prehistory.* Ames: Iowa State University Press, 1975.
(Extensive popular discussion of archaeology of western Iowa.)

Daniel, Glyn. *The Idea of Prehistory.* Cleveland, Ohio: The World Publishing Co.,
1963. (General discussion of the History of archaeology.)

Debo, Lewis C. "They Explored the Des Moines River Basin." *Ottumwa Courier,*
30 Dec. 1966, p. 4.

Froning, Myrna. "Work to Save Artifacts Near Saylorville Reservoir." *Des Moines
Register,* 29 Sept. 1974, p. 8C.

Gradwohl, David M. "Archaeology of the Central Des Moines River Valley: A
Preliminary Summary." In *Aspects of Upper Great Lakes Anthropology.* Edited by
Eldon Johnson, pp. 90–102. Minnesota Historical Society: St. Paul, 1974.
(Detailed discussion of the archaeology of central Iowa with an extensive
bibliography.)

Gradwohl, David M., and Osborn, Nancy. *Stalking the Skunk.* Papers in
Anthropology, Number 1, Iowa State University, 1972. (Archaeological
survey of the Ames Reservoir.)

Grissel, Lois Anna. *An Analysis of a Prehistoric Village Site near Cedar Rapids, Iowa.*
Unpublished M.A. thesis, State University of Iowa, 1946.

Herold, Elaine Bluhm. "Hopewell: Burial Mound Builders." *Palimpsest* 51 (Dec.
1970). (Entire issue is devoted to Woodland Tradition, ca. 200 B.C. to A.D. 400.)

Jennings, Jesse D. *Prehistory of North America.* New York: McGraw-Hill Book Co.,
1968. (A good general outline of the archaeology of North America from
Mexico to the Arctic.)

Keyes, Charles Reuben. *Palimpsest* 32 (Aug. 1951). (Entire issue devoted to
prehistoric cultures in Iowa as known in 1950.)

———. "Indian Rock Shelters." *Palimpsest* 24 (Jan. 1943): 8–15.

Logan, Wilfred David. "Analysis of Woodland Complexes in Northeastern Iowa."
Unpublished Ph.D. dissertation, University of Michigan, 1959.

Logan, Wilfred David, and Ingmanson, J. Earl. "Effigy Mounds National
Monument." *Palimpsest* 50 (May 1969): 273–304.

McKusick, Marshall. *The Davenport Conspiracy*. Iowa City: Office of the State Archaeologist, 1970. (Discussion regarding the manufacture of fake artifacts in the nineteenth century.)

————. *Men of Ancient Iowa*. Ames: Iowa State University Press, 1964. (General discussion of Iowa archaeology as known in 1960.)

Mallam, R. Clark. "The Mound Builders: An American Myth." *Journal of the Iowa Archaeological Society* 23 (1976): 145–75. (Article deals with the evolution of the myth of the lost mound builders.)

Mott, Mildred. "The Relation of Historic Indian Tribes and Archaeological Manifestation in Iowa." *Iowa Journal of History and Politics* 36 (July 1938): 227–304. (Excellent discussion of relationship of archaeological evidence and historically known Indian groups.)

Patterson, Thomas C. *America's Past: A New World Archaeology*. Glenview, Ill.: Scott, Foresman and Co., 1973. (Brief discussion of New World archaeology.)

Sanders, William, and Marino, Joseph. *New World Prehistory: Archaeology of the American Indian*. Englewood Cliffs, N.J.: Prentice-Hall, 1970.

Stone, Larry. "Indians Thrived in Iowa River 'Greenbelt.'" *Des Moines Register*, 15 Sept. 1974, p. 9D.

Wedel, Mildred Mott. "Ethnohistory: Its Payoffs and Pitfalls for Iowa Archaeologists." *Journal of the Iowa Archaeological Society* 23 (1976): 1–44. (Article summarizes the strengths and weaknesses of early archival data pertaining to Iowa history.)

Wedel, Waldo R. *Prehistoric Man on the Great Plains*. Norman: University of Oklahoma Press, 1961. (Best general discussion of archaeology of the Plains.)

Willey, Gordon R. *An Introduction to American Archaeology: North and Middle America*. Vol. 1. Englewood Cliffs, N.J.: Prentice-Hall, 1966. (A general summary of the prehistory of North and Middle America as known from archaeology.)

Willey, Gordon R., and Sabloff, Jeremy A. *A History of American Archaeology*. San Francisco: W. H. Freeman & Co., 1974. (Book deals with changing intellectual and methodological approaches in New World archaeology.)

AUDIO AND VISUAL AIDS

Records

"Authentic Music of the American Indian." Everest Records, 10902 Wilshire Boulevard, Suite 210, Los Angeles, Calif. 90024.

"Crow Dog's Paradise: Songs of the Sioux." Electra Records, 15 Columbus Circle, New York, N.Y. 10023.

"Folk Voices of Iowa." Recorded by Harry Oster. University of Iowa Press, Iowa City, Iowa 52240.

"Healing Songs of the American Indians." Folkways Records, 43 West 61st, New York, N.Y. 10023.

"Oklahoma Indian Chants." Recorded by Louis Ballard. Southwest Music
Publications, 136 West 52nd Street, New York, N.Y. 10019.
"Sioux." Library of Congress Music Division. Washington, D.C. 20540.
"Songs and Dances of the Great Lakes Indians." Recorded by Gertrude Prokosh
Kurath. Ethnic Folkways Library, 43 West 61st, New York, N.Y. 10023.
(Includes Mesquakie songs.)
"War Dance Songs." Recorded by the Mesquakie Bear Singers of Tama, Iowa.
Canyon Records, Phoenix, Ariz. 85012.

Slides and Films
Ancient Iowa Film Series *(Visiting the Indians with George Catlin, Prehistoric Cultures,*
Late Woodland Village, Mill Creek Village People, Earth Lodge People, Oneota
Longhouse People, Fort Madison Archaeology). Iowa City: Office of the State
Archaeologist, 1974–75.
Iowa State Extension. *Iowa's Indian Heritage: Then and Now.* Ames: Iowa State
University, 1973. (Slides and tape available from county extension offices.)
Weber, Alan, and Bartell, Michael. "Mesquakie." Ames: Iowa State University,
1976. (Filmed at 1975 Mesquakie Powwow and includes photographs from the
Iowa State Historical Society.)

BIBLIOGRAPHIES AND DIRECTORIES
A Bibliography of American Indian Materials. Tama, Iowa: Community School District
of South Tama County, 1974. (Elementary and secondary classroom and library
materials.)
Dockstader, Frederick J. *The American Indian in Graduate Studies: A Bibliography of*
Theses and Dissertations. New York: Museum of the American Indian, 1957.
Guide to Implementing Multicultural Non-sexist Curriculum Programs in Iowa Schools. Des
Moines: Iowa Department of Public Instruction, 1976.
Hargrett, L. *A Bibliography of the Constitutions and Laws of the American Indians.*
Cambridge, Mass.: Harvard University Press, 1947.
Indian Historian Press. *Index to Literature on the American Indian.* San Francisco:
Indian Historian Press, 1971, 1972, 1973, 1974.
Klein, Barry T., and Icolari, Dan, eds. *Reference Encyclopedia of the American Indian.*
2 vols. Rye, N.Y.: Todd Publications, 1973–74. (Lists museums, government
publications, visual aids, tribes, and urban centers.)
Multi-cultural, Non-sexist Curriculum Guidelines for Iowa Schools. Des Moines: Iowa
Department of Public Instruction, 1975.
Murdock, G. P. *Ethnographic Bibliography of North America.* 3rd ed. New Haven,
Conn.: Human Relations Area Files, 1960.
Owen, R. C.; Deetz, J. J. F.; and Fisher, A. D. *The North American Indians: A Source*
Book. New York: Macmillan, 1967.

Pratt, LeRoy G. *Discovering Historic Iowa*. Des Moines: Iowa Department of Public
Instruction, 1975. (Arranged by counties and lists historical societies, museums,
and landmarks in each county.)

INDIAN ORGANIZATIONS IN IOWA
(current as of November 1999)
American Indian and Native Studies Program
    404 Jefferson Building
    University of Iowa
    Iowa City, Iowa 52242
American Indian Council Employment and Training Program
    2508 East 4th Street
    Sioux City, Iowa 51101
American Indian Student Association (AISA)
    University of Iowa
    308 Melrose Avenue
    Iowa City, Iowa 52242
American Indian Studies Program
    347 Catt Hall
    Iowa State University
    Ames, Iowa 50011
American Indian Science and Engineering Society (AISES)
    301 Beardshear Hall
    Iowa State University
    Ames, Iowa 50011
American Indian Science and Engineering Society (AISES)
    308 Melrose Avenue
    Iowa City, Iowa 52242
American Indian Rights Organization (AIRO)
    301 Beardshear Hall
    Iowa State University
    Ames, Iowa 50011
Department of History, Indian Studies, and Political Science
    Morningside College
    Sioux City, Iowa 51106
Indian Youth of America, Inc.
    609 Badgerow Building
    Sioux City, Iowa 51101
Latino/Native American Cultural Center (LNACC)
    308 Melrose Avenue
    Iowa City, Iowa 52242

Meskwaki Alcohol Drug Abuse Center
   1826 430th Street
   Tama, Iowa 52339
Meskwaki Bingo and Casino
   Highway 30
   Tama, Iowa 52339
Meskwaki Healthy Start
   349 Meskwaki Road
   Tama, Iowa 52339
Meskwaki Senior Services
   RR #2
   Tama, Iowa 52339
Meskwaki Training Center
   1496 Highway 30
   Tama, Iowa 52339
Native American Alcohol Treatment Center
   P.O. Box 790-A
   Sergeant Bluff, Iowa 51054
Native American Child Care Center
   1735 Morningside Avenue
   Sioux City, Iowa 51106
Native American Student Union
   Center for Multicultural Education
   University of Northern Iowa
   Cedar Falls, IA 50614-0395
Native American Law Students Association (NALSA)
   Boyd Law Building
   University of Iowa
   Iowa City, Iowa 52242
Office of Indian Education
   P.O. Box 1113
   Sioux City, Iowa 51102-1113
Sac and Fox Tribe of the Mississippi in Iowa
   (Meskwaki Tribal Offices)
   349 Meskwaki Road
   Tama, Iowa 52339
Sioux City American Indian Center
   610 13th Street, Suite B
   Sioux City, Iowa 51105
Sioux City Healthy Start
   809 West 7th Street
   Sioux City, Iowa 51103

Title IX Indian Education Project
   Sioux City Community Schools
   1221 Pierce Street
   Sioux City, Iowa 51105
United Native American Student Association (UNASA)
   301 Beardshear Hall
   Iowa State University
   Ames, Iowa 50011

OTHER RESOURCES
Bureau of Indian Affairs
   1951 Constitution Avenue, N.W.
   Washington, D.C. 20402
Iowa Archaeological Society
   Office of the State Archaeologist
   University of Iowa
   Iowa City, Iowa 52242
Iowa Civil Rights Commission
   211 East Maple Street
   Des Moines, Iowa 50309
Iowa Tribe of Kansas and Nebraska
   P.O. Box 58A, Route 1
   White Cloud, Kansas 66094
Office of the State Archaeologist
   University of Iowa
   Iowa City, Iowa 52242
Omaha Tribe of Nebraska
   P.O. Box 368
   Macy, Nebraska 68039
State Historical Society of Iowa
   600 East Locust Street
   Des Moines, Iowa 50319
Winnebago Tribe of Nebraska
   P.O. Box 687
   Winnebago, Nebraska 68071

Selected Updated Bibliography

Alex, Lynn Marie. *Iowa's Archaeological Past*. Iowa City: University of Iowa Press, 2000. (The most comprehensive, up-to-date summary available for the prehistory and early history of Native Americans in Iowa.)

———. *Exploring Iowa's Past: A Guide to Prehistoric Archaeology*. Iowa City: University of Iowa Press, 1980.

Anderson, Duane. *Mill Creek Ceramics: The Complex from the Brewster Site*. Iowa City: Office of the State Archaeologist, University of Iowa, 1981.

Behrman, Sara. "Selected Sources on the Mesquakie Indians." Research Papers, Office of the State Archaeologist, University of Iowa 8,1 (1983).

Blaine, Martha Royce. *The Ioway Indians*. Norman: University of Oklahoma Press, 1995. (Paperback edition with new preface by the author; originally published 1979.)

Blakeslee, Donald J., ed. *The Central Plains Tradition: Internal Development and External Relationships*. Iowa City: Office of the State Archaeologist, University of Iowa, 1978.

Callender, Charles. "Fox." In *Northeast*, edited by Bruce Trigger. *Handbook of North American Indians* 15 (1978): 636–47. Washington, D.C.: Smithsonian Institution.

Dahlstrom, Amy. Special Issue on Fox. *Contemporary Linguistics* 2 (1996). University of Chicago, Department of Linguistics. (Contemporary essays on Fox / Meskwaki linguistics.)

Davis, Mary B, ed. *Native America in the Twentieth Century: An Encyclopedia*. New York: Garland Publishing, 1994.

Edmunds, R. David. "Mesquaki." In *Native America in the Twentieth Century: An Encyclopedia*. Mary B. Davis, ed. Pp. 336–37. New York: Garland Publishing, 1994.

Edmunds, R. David and Joseph L. Peyser. *The Fox Wars: The Mesquakie Challenge to New France*. Norman; University of Oklahoma Press, 1993.

Fargo, O. *Iowa Indians: Book 2*. Creston, IA: Green Valley Area Education Agency 14, 1988.

Fikes, Jay O. *Reuben Snake, Your Humble Servant. Indian Visionary and Activist*, as told to Jay C. Fikes. Santa Fe, NM. Clear Light Publishers, 1996.

Foley, Douglas E. *The Heartland Chronicles*. Philadelphia: University of Pennsylvania Press, 1995. (Deals with the Meskwaki from the perspective of an anthropologist who grew up in Tama, Iowa. Uses pseudonyms even when referring to published works by Ray Young Bear and Donald Wanatee.)

Foster, Lance M. "The Ioway and the Lost Landscape of Southeast Iowa." *Journal of the Iowa Archeological Society* 43 (1996): 1–5.

————. *Mayan Jegi (This Land Here): The Ioway Indians and the Lost Landscape of Iowa*. M.L.A. Creative Component, Iowa State University, 1997.

————. *Sacred Bundles of the Iowa Indians*. M.A. Thesis, Iowa State University, 1994.

Gourley, Kathryn E. *Locations of Sauk, Mesquakie, and Associated Euro-American Sites 1832–1845: An Ethnohistoric Approach*. M.A. Thesis, Iowa State University, 1990.

Gradwohl, David M. "Shelling Corn in the Prairies and Plains: Archaeological Evidence and Ethnographic Parallels beyond the Pun." In *Plains Indian Studies: A Collection of Essays in Honor of John C. Ewers and Waldo R. Wedel*. Douglas H. Ubelaker and Herman J. Viola, eds. Pp. 135–56. Smithsonian Contributions to Anthropology No. 30. Washington, DC: Smithsonian Institution Press, 1982.

Green, William. *Agricultural Origins and Development in the Midcontinent*. Iowa City: Office of the State Archaeologist, University of Iowa, 1994.

Green, William, David W. Benn, and Robert Boszhardt. *Oneota Archaeology: Past, Present, and Future*. Iowa City: University of Iowa Press, 1995.

Greenwood, Stanley James. *A Mesquakie Document*. M.A. Thesis, University of Iowa, 1974.

Guggenheim, Charles (producer and director), Mayo Simon, and Dick Hartzell. "The Whole Town's Talking." Ames, IA: WOI-TV, 1952. (Television production featuring members of the Mesquakie tribe discussing the future of the settlement school. Available only at the Iowa State University Library.)

Hagen, William Thomas. *The Sac and Fox Indians*. Norman: University of Oklahoma Press, 1988.

Harrington, Mark. *Sacred Bundles of the Sac and Fox Indians*. New York: AMS Press, 1983.

Harvey, Amy E. *Oneota Culture in Northwestern Iowa*. Iowa City: Office of the State Archaeologist, University of Iowa, 1979.

Hirschfelder, Arlene and Martha Kreipe de Montaño. *The Native American Almanac: A Portrait of Native America Today*. New York: Prentice Hall, 1993. (A general reference source.)

Hoover, Herbert T. *The Yankton Sioux*. New York: Chelsea House Publishers, 1988.

"Iowa" [Ioway Tribe]. In *Native America in the Twentieth Century: An Encyclopedia*. Mary B. Davis, ed. Pp. 276–77. New York: Garland Publishing, 1994.

Irwin, Hadley. *We are Mesquakie, We are One*. Old Westbury, NY: Feminist Press, 1980.

Kurtz, Royce Delbert. *Economic and Political History of the Sauk and Mesquakie, 1780s–1845*. Ph.D. Dissertation, University of Iowa, 1986.

Lacey, Theresa, Nancy Bonvillain, Frank W. Porter, eds. *The Sac and Fox*. New York: Chelsea House, 1995.

Laird, Allison. *A Guide to Native American Artifacts in Iowa Hall*. Iowa City: University of Iowa Press, 1990.

Lee, L. P. *History of the Spirit Lake Massacre*. Rpt. Fairfield, WA: Ye Galleon Press, 1996.

Logan, Wilfred David. *Woodland Complexes in Northeastern Iowa.* Washington, D.C.:
    U.S. Department of the Interior, National Park Service, 1976.

Lurie, Nancy Oestreich. "Winnebago." In *Northeast,* edited by Bruce Trigger.
    Handbook of North American Indians 15 (1978): 690–707. Washington, D.C.:
    Smithsonian Institution.

"Problems of the Urban Indian." New York: Clearwater Publishing, 1981.
    (Recording of George Sun discussing problems facing Native Americans in
    Sioux City and Oscar Howe describing his experiences in a federal boarding
    school.)

Reinschmidt, Michael. *Ethnohistory of the Sauk, 1885–1985: A Socio-political Study on
    Continuity and Change.* Gottingen [Germany]: Cuvillier, 1993.

Ruzicki, Gerald Matthew. "Health and the Mesquakie Indians." M.A. Thesis,
    University of Iowa, 1970.

Schwieder, Dorothy. *Iowa: The Middle Land.* Ames: Iowa State University Press,
    1996.

———, Lynn Nielsen, and Thomas J. Morain. *Iowa: Past to Present, the People and the
    Prairie.* Ames: Iowa State University Press, 1991.

Sprengel, Lisa Lynn. *The Nutrient Intake and Nutrition Knowledge of the Elderly
    Mesquakie Indians.* M.A. Thesis, University of Iowa, 1984.

Tama News Herald Staff. *The History of Tama County Iowa.* Dallas: Curtis Media,
    1987.

Theler, James L. *Woodland Tradition Economic Strategies: Animal Resource Utilization in
    Southwestern Wisconsin and Northeastern Iowa.* Iowa City: University of Iowa Press,
    1987.

Tiffany, Joseph A. *Chan-ya-ta: A Mill Creek Village.* Iowa City: Office of the State
    Archaeologist, University of Iowa, 1982.

——— and Duane Anderson. "The Milford Site (13DKi): A Post-Contact
    Oneota Village in Northwest Iowa." Memoir 27, *Plains Anthropologist* 38, 145
    (1993): 283–306.

Torrence, Gaylord and Robert Hobbs. *Art of the Red Earth People, The Mesquakie of
    Iowa.* Seattle: University of Washington Press, 1989.

United States Commission on Civil Rights, Iowa Advisory Committee. *Race
    Relations in Tama County: A Report.* Washington, D.C.: The U.S. Commission on
    Civil Rights, 1981.

United States Indian Claims Commission. *Commission Findings on the Sac, Fox, and
    Iowa Indians.* New York: Garland, 1974.

VanStone, James W. *Mesquakie (Fox) Material Culture: The William Jones and Frederick
    Starr Collections.* Chicago: Field Museum of Natural History, 1998.

Vogel, Virgil. *Iowa Place Names of Indian Origin.* Iowa City: University of Iowa Press,
    1963.

Wedel, Mildred Mott. "Peering at the Ioway Indians through the Mist of Time:
    1650–circa 1700." *Journal of the Iowa Archeological Society* 33 (1986): 1–74.

Young Bear, Ray A. *Black Eagle Child: The Facepaint Narratives.* Iowa City: University of Iowa Press, 1992.

————. *The Invisible Musician.* Duluth, MN: Holy Cow! Press, 1990.

————. *Remnants of the First Earth.* New York: Grove/Atlantic, 1997.

————. *Winter of the Salamander: The Keeper of Importance.* San Francisco: Harper and Row, 1980.

Notes on Contributors

Gretchen M. Bataille is senior vice president of Academic Affairs for the University of North Carolina system. She was formerly in the Department of English at Iowa State University, where she taught American Indian literature. She is the author, with Charles L. P. Silet, of *The Pretend Indians* and, with Kathleen M. Sands, of *American Indian Women, Telling Their Lives*.

Lance M. Foster, an Ioway Indian (Baxoje), obtained a B.A. in anthropology and American Indian Studies from the University of Montana. He studied painting and sketching at the Institute of American Indian Arts in Santa Fe before completing two masters degrees at Iowa State University: one in anthropology and one in landscape architecture. In 1997 Foster founded Native Nations Press. He lives in Santa Fe, where he works for the Cultural Landscapes Program of the National Park Service.

David Mayer Gradwohl is professor emeritus of Anthropology at Iowa State University and former chair of the university's American Indian Studies Program. His specific interest in the prehistory of the prairie-plains regions goes back to his undergraduate days at the University of Nebraska. He is the author of *Exploring Buried Buxton* and an article on Kiowa Caddo

artist T. C. Cannon in the journal *Markers*.

Donald Graham was previously director of the American Indian Council's alcoholism treatment center in Sergeant Bluff, Iowa. He now lives in Aberdeen, South Dakota, where he is employed by the Indian Health Service.

Joseph Hraba is professor of sociology at Iowa State University, where he teaches classes on ethnicity in the United States and conducts research on ethnicity, economic, and health issues in this country as well as in Europe and Asia.

Michael Husband taught history at Morningside College in Sioux City, Iowa, where he was instrumental in acquiring a grant for an Indian Studies program. He participated in a research project on American Indian oral history at the University of New Mexico, and has worked in historical museums both in Arizona and Colorado.

Gary Koerselman taught history at Morningside College in Sioux City, Iowa, and was involved in the Indian Studies Institute. A specialist in twentieth-century American history, he served on the Iowa Civil Rights Commission from 1972 to 1976 and was appointed in 1976 to the Iowa Educational Radio and Television Facility Board. He died in 1988.

Owana McLester-Greenfield, a Shoshone, served as Native American Coordinator for Drake University, Des Moines Area Community College, and Grandview College. She now teaches literature at Simpson College in Indianola, Iowa, and is the owner of the Mastery Company, which specializes in communications training. In 1993 she received the Outstanding Adult Educator of Iowa award.

Fred McTaggart received his Ph.D. from the University of Iowa and pursued his interest in the literature of the American Indian during his fellowship at the Center for the History of the American Indian at the Newberry Library in Chicago. He taught at Western Michigan University before opening his own business writing health-care articles for hospitals. In 1993 he wrote a review of Ray Young Bear's *Black Eagle Child* for the *Annals of Iowa*.

Maria D. Pearson is a political activist, an advisor for programs involving Native American education, and a consultant on cultural preservation and repatriation issues. A member of the Turtle Clan of the Yankton Sioux tribe, she has chaired the Indian Advisory Committee for the Office of the State Archaeologist since 1974. She helped organize the World Archaeological Congress's First Inter-Congress on the Disposition of the Dead in 1989.

L. Edward Purcell was formerly a staff member at the State Historical Society in Iowa City, where he was editor of the *Palimpsest*. He is a gradu-

ate of Simpson College and the University of Iowa. After teaching history at Transylvania University, he became a freelance writer of educational references. He lives in Lexington, Kentucky, and is the author or co-author of sixteen books.

Charles L. P. Silet is a professor in the English Department at Iowa State University where he teaches, does research, and publishes on contemporary fiction, culture, and film. His latest books are *The Critical Response to Chester Himes* and *Talking Murder: 20 Interviews with Mystery and Crime Writers*.

Reuben Snake was the former director of the Indian Education Project in Sioux City. After his death in 1993, his life's story was published under the title *Reuben Snake, Your Humble Serpent*.

Adeline Wanatee spent most of her life at the Meskwaki Settlement near Tama. She was educated at the Flandreau Indian School in South Dakota and Haskell Institute in Lawrence, Kansas. The first Native American to be inducted into the Iowa Women's Hall of Fame, she began her Spirit Journey in 1996.

Donald Wanatee, as a student at Iowa State University, helped found the United Native American Student Association. He completed a master's degree in social work at the University of Iowa and served as the Meskawki tribe's executive director. He has served as a member of the Coalition of Indian-Controlled School Boards and as a fellow of the Robert H. Kennedy

Foundation. He now resides at the Meskwaki settlement with his wife and some of his children and grandchildren.

Duren J. H. Ward, a Canadian educated at Hillsdale College, Harvard University, and Leipzig University, was a Unitarian minister, lecturer, and anthropologist in Iowa City at the turn of the century. Under the auspices of the State Historical Society, he undertook a systematic recording of the history and culture of the Meskwaki. He died in 1942.

Bertha Waseskuk, who began her Spirit Journey in 1979, was a member of the Meskwaki tribe. Her essay in the first edition of this book has been acknowledged as a valuable expression of Meskwaki oral historical knowledge that has been handed down through the generations.

Index

racism, 34, 100, 101, 132, 145, 153
Radin, Paul, 2, 3
Ray, Robert D., 132, 134–138, 140
Red Earth People, 22, 42. *See also* Fox;
Mesquakie
The Red Men of Iowa, 26
Reida, Bernice, 22
religions, Indian, 117, 118
Renard, 42, 63, 83. *See also* Fox;
Mesquakie
Rhodd, Benjamin K. (Potawatami), 131
Rousseau, John Jacques, 11
Rummells-Maske Site, 42
Running Moccasins. *See* Maria Pearson

Sac (tribe), 64, 66, 83, 85, 87, 120, 123,
125, 145, 153. *See also* Fox; Sauk
Sac and Fox Housing Authority, 116
Sac and Fox Tribal Council, 116
Sac Savagism and Civilization, 11
"Sacred Bundles of the Ioway Indians,"
146
Sainte-Marie, Buffy (Cree), 10
Santee (Sioux), 42, 53, 90, 108, 109, 113,
128
Sauk/Sac, 19, 20, 21, 25, 53, 64, 142,
145, 154. *See also* Sac
Seven Arrows, 6
Silverberg, Robert, 40
Siouan (language), 18, 53
Sioux City, 56, 89, 90, 91, 108, 109–110,
112–116, 119, 137, 152, 154
Sioux, Oglala, 79, 94
Sioux (tribe), 14, 18, 19, 35, 42, 90, 113,
131, 132, 145
Sitting Bull (Hunkpapa Sioux), 114, 128
South Dakota, 131
Spirit Journey, 132, 133, 136, 137, 141
Spirit Lake, 110
Spirit Lake Massacre, 19, 21, 22, 23
Spirits of Our Old People (*S'ageh*), 146,
147, 148

Standing Bear, Luther (Oglala Sioux),
30, 31, 34, 79, 94
Stanislaw, Pete (Flathead), 116
State Historical Society of Iowa, 24,
25, 39
stereotypes
in curriculum, 17–28
in film, 14, 15
in literature, 25
in textbooks, 19–24
Sterns, Kay, 134
Stories of Iowa Boys and Girls, 24
Storm, Chuck, 6
Strange Empire, 17
subsistence, 42–52, 61

Tama County, 22, 54, 56, 66, 67, 112,
123, 152
Tama, Iowa, 4, 18, 22, 23, 94, 100, 116,
152
Tatanga Mani (Stoney), 1
Tedlock, Dennis, 6
Tell a Tale of Iowa, 23
Tep-pes-su-pen-a-hut (Mesquakie), 66
This Is the Place, Iowa, 19
Thomas, Anthony (Winnebago), 116
Thunder (clan), 143, 146
Toledo, Iowa, 23
Trail of Broken Treaties, 152
treaties, 17, 20, 63, 64
tribal governments, 79–88
tribes. *See* individual tribal names
Trickster, 146–147
Two Elk, Aaron (Ogalala Sioux), 116

unemployment, 91
United States Constitution, 81
University of Iowa, 6
University of Nebraska, 121
Upper Iowa River, 142, 144, 147
urbanization, 110
The Uses of the Past, 55